More Praise for
"Chuck" vs. the Business World

"Obviously, my friend, Ray Keating, has too much free time. The good news is Ray has lurched uncontrollably to producing the most relevant, instructive and entertaining book ever written for both small business owners and spies. If you're either of these – or want to be – don't miss this. Who knows? You might even find a new calling."

- Jim Blasingame
Small Business Expert and Host of
The Small Business Advocate® Show

"Chuck"
vs. the
Business World

....

Business Tips on TV

Ray Keating

This book has not been approved, licensed, or sponsored by any entity or person involved in creating or producing *Chuck* the television series.

Keating Reports, LLC
P.O. Box 596
Manorville, NY 11934
keatingreports@aol.com

ISBN-13: 978-1466345713

ISBN-10: 1466345713

For
Jonathan, David and Beth

Previous Books by Ray Keating

Warrior Monk: A Pastor Stephen Grant Novel (2010)

Discussion Guide for Warrior Monk:
A Pastor Stephen Grant Novel (2011)

U.S. by the Numbers:
What's Left, Right, and Wrong with America State by State
(2000)

New York by the Numbers:
State and City in Perpetual Crisis (1997)

D.C. by the Numbers: A State of Failure (1995)

Table of Contents

1. The Boss Versus the Workers?
An Introduction   1

2. The Buy More Versus the Customer:
Is the Customer Always Right?   7

3. "Jeffster" Versus the Buy More:
Who Works for You?   12

4. The General Versus Big Mike:
Who's the Boss?   16

5. Chuck Versus Chuck:
Which Chuck Are You?   23

6. Chuck Versus The Intersect:
Is Technology Your Friend or Foe?   28

7. Chuck Versus Leadership?
Leading to Get Things Done   33

8. Chuck Versus the Cheese Balls:
Dealing with Failure   37

9. Chuck Versus the Not-So-Dream Job?
Losing the Dream Job   41

10. John Casey Versus Daniel Shaw:
Company Man Versus Company Turncoat   45

11. Chuck Versus Communication:
Communicating in the Workplace   50

12. Casey Versus Sarah?
Developing a Partnership   53

13. Trust Versus Work?
Co-Workers, Employees and Bosses 58

14. The Business Versus Jeffster:
Sex, Drugs, Gambling, Booze and
Violence in the Workplace 65

15. Casey Versus the Business Plan:
Changing the Mission 70

16. The Buy More Versus Employee Pay:
How *Not* to Compensate or Motivate Your People 77

17. The Buy More Versus Wasting Talent:
The Hannah Example 82

18. The NSA Versus Employee Training:
Casey on Training Workers 86

19. Business Versus the Number Two Guy:
Harry, Morgan, Lester and Emmett 90

20. Lou Versus Lester:
The Passion of the Entrepreneur 94

21. The CIA Versus Love:
Love in the Workplace 97

22. Chuck Versus the Interview:
The Angst of Interviews 103

23. The Buy More Versus the CIA:
Terminating Employees 107

24. Sales Versus the Buy More:
Advertising and Sales Strategies 112

25. Morgan Versus Courage:
The Big Moments 116

26. Personal Life Versus Work Life:
Keeping Work in Perspective   120

27. A Salute to "Chuck" for Family and Business   125

About the Author   130

"...strong enough to bend like the reed and not snap like the Kit Kat...?"

- Big Mike

1
The Boss Versus the Workers? An Introduction

Okay, admit it. At some point in your career, you've worked with, worked for, or managed people who were so annoying or inept that you wanted to just slam their heads together – like Batman might do with a couple of the Joker's henchmen.

But with an inevitable lawsuit looming, not to mention possible criminal charges, hopefully, you never acted on the impulse.

The idea for this book came while watching an episode of the NBC television series *Chuck* in which a character does exactly that, i.e., grabs two troublesome workers and bangs their heads together. Not only was it darn funny, but it also got me thinking about business tips – lessons on what to do and what not to do in the business world – that might be derived from this television show. As a writer, economist for a small business group, and an adjunct college professor in an MBA program, I'm always trying to think of new and improved ways to communicate and educate.

Before I get to this particular head-banging incident, however, let's set the stage by quickly summing up what *Chuck* is all about, who the key players are, and why the show lends itself to providing some career and business insights.

Chuck is part comedy, part spy drama focused around Chuck Bartowski (played by Zachary Levi). The show lands somewhere between James Bond and *Get Smart*. As the series started out, Chuck was a smart, nerdy guy, but an underachiever in his job as part of the Nerd Herd (kind of like the Geek Squad?) at the Buy More, a large electronics store (similar to Best Buy?).

In addition, he was not exactly knocking them dead in his personal life. For example, when we first meet Chuck at his birthday party, he tells assorted women that his chaffed fingers are due to hours of playing the video game *Call of Duty*. Not surprisingly, they seem unimpressed.

But life unexpectedly changes when Chuck winds up with a computer – the Intersect – with massive amounts of government information implanted in his head courtesy of an e-mail from an old college friend turned spy. As Chuck puts it: "Yesterday, I was making eleven bucks an hour fixing computers, now I have one in my brain."

The Intersect ushers two spies into his life. Sarah Walker (portrayed by Yvonne Strahovski) is the beautiful, but deadly CIA agent. Meanwhile, John Casey (played by Adam Baldwin) is a "cold school" assassin for the NSA. The three become "Team Bartowski," reporting to General Diane Beckman (Bonita Friedericy).

Chuck's home life features his worrying sister Ellie Bartowski (Sarah Lancaster) and her significant other Devon "Captain Awesome" Woodcomb (Ryan McPartlin). Both are doctors.

Despite the Intersect and his new spy life, Chuck's Buy More job continues as a cover. His best friend, and fellow underachiever, Morgan Grimes (Joshua Gomez), is a co-worker, along with two creepy individuals – Jeff Barnes (Scott Krinsky) and Lester Patel (Vik Sahay) – who also have a struggling, lousy band named "Jeffster." The Buy More usually is guided, to use the word very loosely, by the hands-off managerial style of Big Mike (Mark Christopher Lawrence).

Over the first four seasons, other players entered and exited this dysfunctional, slothful and perhaps not-all-that-unusual workplace.

With some wonderful, insightful comedy, the team creating, writing and producing *Chuck* has provided a wealth of examples on how *not* to manage a business, and how *not* to behave in the workplace. We all learn not only from our own mistakes and failures, but also from the mistakes and failures of others. Business case literature is as rich with examples of bad decisions and failure as with successes in the marketplace. By climbing into *Chuck*, however, I found a few valuable positives as well. Overall, *Chuck* offers tips covering a wide range of areas, including day-to-day business management and operations, career choices, and the balance and priorities that must be established between work and personal life.

Early in my own career, I worked for an individual who had tremendous talent in his field of expertise, but also possessed an enormous ego and absolutely no skills at managing his employees and generally relating to others. I tried to gain from the positives, and avoid the negatives.

Now, let's get back to that head-banging moment in *Chuck*. It ties in to one of the oldest problems in business: Are the employees and management working together, or against each other? (Season 3, Episode 11: "Chuck Versus the Final Exam")

Considering that labor and capital – or employees and owners – need each other, and must work together in order to succeed, the notion that the workers and the managers/owners are opponents should be an economic and business absurdity. Of course, though, plenty of absurdities win out over basic common sense in life.

In this particular episode, Jeff and Lester are chasing each other around the Buy More with Nerf target guns, oblivious to work, and knocking into and over customers. Casey, filling in as assistant manager and having lost his NSA job, is not pleased, and grabs the two.

Casey tells them: "Together, you constitute a clear and present danger to the store, who need to be neutralized."

Lester challenges Casey, and informs him of the "no touching policy here at the store, granted it's mostly for Jeff, but it holds company wide." He further taunts Casey: "Don't you see, Johnny, you can't harm us thanks to the rules of the very corporate system you so admire. Ha, the irony."

Casey responds, "I love irony." He knocks their heads together, they topple to the floor, and he walks away.

Big Mike, the Buy More manager, calls Casey into the office, while Lester and Jeff are holding ice packs to their heads, demanding justice and a "humiliating apology." During the meeting, Casey writes on his hand, "I am going to kill you," shows it to Jeff and Lester, further frightening them. They scramble from the office, promising lawsuits.

Big Mike finally asks Casey: "What I need to know is are you mentally strong, strong enough to bend like the reed and not snap like the Kit Kat, to be John Casey not John Crazy?"

Later, Big Mike, being fitted for a new suit in the Buy More office by his tailor, tells Casey that he has assured Jeff and Lester that Casey could change. How? Big Mike advises Casey: "To get your head right, you have to get your threads right."

With a new suit, Casey admits to feeling "pretty good," and apologizes to and promises Jeff and Lester that he will no longer bang them around. Casey seals the deal by having to eat the same disgusting sandwich that repulsive Jeff was eating.

All of this, of course, was done to avoid a potential lawsuit brought by employees.

Chuck Business Tips

Despite the glaring reality that workers and management/ownership must work together to get ahead, it remains a constant challenge in business to get everyone to accept the firm's mission and work to achieve its objectives.

In this *Chuck* example, all the wrong people seem to be in the mix.

Jeff and Lester care nothing about pleasing Buy More customers. And it's impossible to picture any scenario whereby they might change. Unfortunately, sometimes the only correct answer is to fire those unwilling to work. Cut your losses. We'll see some examples later in the book.

As for Casey, while he correctly identifies employees like Jeff and Lester as threats to the well being of the business, he possesses none of the managerial skills necessary to deal with the situation in an appropriate manner. And because he does not have the training and temperament to manage, Casey places the business and himself at risk of being taken to court.

Finally, as store manager, Big Mike does nothing to improve the workplace or provide incentives for employees to work towards common goals and objectives. Putting aside his own misuse of work time for the moment (and that's no small matter), when trouble arrives, he avoids the necessary decisions, and instead, does the bare minimum to gloss over or just get by the current situation. His solutions are superficial and temporary, rather than substantive and transformative.

The result? A workplace of "us against them," and a recipe for business failure. It's critical that owners and managers clearly communicate the firm's mission, and establish incentives so that everyone works together to achieve clear goals that make sense.

When Using this Book

When referencing examples and dialogue from the Chuck *television series, I include the season in which the episode ran, the episode number, and the episode title for those wishing to watch those particular moments. This can lend itself to discussion and analysis of particular situations, and debating possible solutions or benefits. It also happens to be quite enjoyable.*

"I'm sorry, I'm on a break."

- Morgan

2
The Buy More Versus the Customer: Is the Customer Always Right?

It's the old saw about business: The customer is always right.

While people can complain about the choices made in the marketplace, if you want to succeed in business and in your career, you better make sure that your customers are happy. Indeed, the point of free enterprise is that entrepreneurs offer new and improved goods and services, businesses compete, and the consumer – the customer – serves as final judge and jury as to what works and what does not.

In the end, the customer must be served and respected.

For the most part, the Buy More in *Chuck* illustrates what *not* to do when it comes to customers.

• Consider two examples when store employees were asked for help.

In one instance, Jeff and Lester, sitting behind the Nerd Herd desk, are trying to find out if Jeff is clairvoyant. A customer, Ellie, seeks assistance and says, "Excuse me." Lester responds, "Damn it, lady, can't you see that you're ruining his concentration?" (Season 4, Episode 18: "Chuck Versus the A-Team")

Similarly, another customer asks, "Excuse me, could I please get some help?" Morgan looks at his watch, does a short countdown, and announces, "I'm sorry, I'm on a break." (Season 1, Episode 9: "Chuck Versus the Imported Hard Salami")

• Of course, there's also the case when customers cannot even find anyone for help. Instead, the Buy More staff is in the employee lounge playing "mystery crisper," wagering on whether Morgan, blindfolded, will eat unknown food from the refrigerator. (Season 1, Episode 6: "Chuck Versus the Sandworm")

• Other examples involve holiday shopping. Black Friday – the big shopping day after Thanksgiving – has been given amusing treatment in *Chuck*. Preparing for the post-Thanksgiving rush, Big Mike gives a speech to Nerd Herd employees. He declares, "I'm talking about Black Friday people, the biggest shopping day of the year, when regular housewives transform into a crazy mob blinded by door prizes, sales, and the urge to get the Christmas shopping done early. On Friday, I'm reassigning you nerds to crowd control." When Morgan is training the herd, he states, "People's lives are at stake." Later he adds, "We cannot lose the doors. Okay, if we lose the doors, we lose the battle." (Season 1, Episode 10: "Chuck Versus the Nemesis")

As for last-minute Christmas shopping, Big Mike arrives at work on Christmas Eve morning at the same time as his assistant manager, Emmett Milbarge (Tony

Hale). They are jubilant. (Season 2, Episode 11: "Chuck Versus Santa Claus")

Riffing on *Apocalypse Now*, Big Mike announces, "Love the smell of day-before-Christmas in the morning."

Emmett responds, "There's just nothing quite like the sweet scent of desperate last-minute shoppers in the air."

Big Mike asks, "You jack our prices up by 10 percent?"

Emmett declares, "Fifteen. You snooze you lose."

Big Mike states, "We're gonna rob them blind."

And they wish each other "Merry Christmas."

• Finally, there is the question of how disappointed customers should be handled. Gamers have packed the store, awaiting the release of a new video game. Morgan, as Buy More manager, is worried about making the release work. He tells Chuck: "Biggest game of the year drops tonight. Okay, and these fanboys have been camped out for a week, a week, without their consoles and simulated killing. You could cut their bloodlust with a knife." But rather than getting hundreds of copies, the Buy More finds out that it is only getting six. Rather than informing the customers, Morgan chooses to delay and misdirect. The crowd grows angrier, and eventually riots when the truth is revealed. (Season 4, Episode 3: "Chuck Versus the Cubic Z")

Chuck Business Tips

Review the actions taken in the above examples: abused or ignored customers seeking assistance; thinking of your customers as a crazy mob; jacking up prices when customers are most vulnerable; or simply failing and then deceiving the customer.

In each of these examples, why would any shopper ever return? To a significant degree, they will not. In a competitive marketplace, alternatives exist. And that most certainly is the case in retail, including the technological reality of being able to shop online from the comfort of home.

So, how does one treat customers in such a market? How does one differentiate? The answer lies with providing quality in terms of product, price and service. And Chuck Bartowski shows the way with a customer in need. (Season 1, Episode 1: "Chuck: The Pilot")

A father fails to put a digital tape in his handheld digital recorder, and therefore misses his daughter's dance recital. He comes to the Nerd Herd for help. Chuck sets up part of the store to recreate and record the scene for the young ballerina. The father is pleased that his wife will not kill him, the girl is happy, and thanks to Chuck going above and beyond, the Buy More has a faithful customer. Add in the fact that other customers saw this touching scene play out in the store, and undoubtedly they will use word of mouth to increase loyalty. Chuck provides valued service, and that matters.

Chuck, in a sense, knew his customer and what was needed. In *The Wall Street Journal Essential Guide to Management* (HarperCollins, New York, 2010), Alan Murray reports:

> Procter & Gamble's former CEO A.G. Lafley ... inherited a company whose culture was criticized for being too insular. He single-handedly changed that culture, in part by insisting company executives spend more time with their customers. Lafley himself would make ten or fifteen such visits with consumers every year, observing women doing everything from washing clothes to applying makeup.

In their classic *In Search of Excellence: Lessons from America's Best-Run Companies* (HarperCollins, New York,

1982), Thomas J. Peters and Robert H. Waterman, Jr. wrote:

> In observing the excellent companies, and specifically the way they interact with customers, what we found most interesting was the consistent presence of *obsession*. This characteristically occurred as a seemingly unjustifiable over commitment to some form of quality, reliability, or service.

Even large, discount retailers cannot afford to fall into the trap of thinking that customer service does not matter at all if their prices are low enough. To varying degrees, of course, it's all about what the customer cares about: both quality *and* price.

"We're staging a revolution to take down the man."

- Lester

3

"Jeffster" Versus the Buy More: Who Works for You?

Employees are both the backbone and the ambassadors of any business. So, the importance of having the right people can in no way be overestimated. And that's not just about employees with certain skills, but with solid character and strong work ethics as well.

In contrast, the wrong employees mean that your business can suffer or even go under. The Buy More in *Chuck* regularly serves up examples of the wrong people for the job.

• When extra work is dumped on the Nerd Herd crew while Chuck is off on a mission, they immediately look to bail. While Morgan urges them to get back to work, they offer lame excuses for leaving, with one herder, Anna Wu (Julia Ling), saying, "Internet poker," and Jeff adding, "I'm off by 8:00 and hammered by 8:05." (Season 1, Episode 3: "Chuck Versus the Tango")

• Assigned to do a double shift at the Buy More, Morgan instead goes AWOL to an arcade to play a video game. (Season 1, Episode 6: "Chuck Versus the Sandworm")

• When Buy More employees believe that another firm is going to purchase the store and fire everyone except Morgan and Chuck, Big Mike and the others lock down the store and barricade themselves in until they get their jobs back. (Season 3, Episode 9: "Chuck Versus the Beard")

Big Mike declares, "These corporate fat cats believe they can take whatever they want. They can take our dignity. They can take all the hot women. But they will not take our jobs. And they will never take our store."

Later, Casey has to enter the store on separate spy business, but the protestors stop him and question his loyalties. Casey asks, "What the hell is going on in here?"

And Jeff responds, "We're staging a revolution to take down the man."

Lester asks Casey: "How do we know we can trust you, son, that you're not some kind of spy for the man?"

Casey's answer: "Because the only thing I hate more than hippie, neo-liberal fascists and anarchists are the hypocrite, fat-cat suits they eventually grow up to become."

Lester says, "Yep, that works for me."

• Morgan tries to tell Big Mike that he is going to quit, and they both wind up crying. When Morgan offers a hug, Big Mike stops him and, referring to his own employees, says, "I can't show emotions like this, those animals out there, they'll get me if I do." (Season 3, Episode 13: "Chuck Versus the Other Guy")

• When managing the Buy More with Halloween approaching, Morgan needs to get the store decorated. He starts out doing it himself, but is overwhelmed. Big Mike offers advice: "After 12-and-a-half weeks at the El Segundo

School of Finance, I learned one very important word: delegate. That word is the key to being a successful manager." Morgan thanks him and asks Big Mike to "dress the Buy More for Halloween." Big Mike turns him down because he is "knee deep in this new Danielle Steel novel." (Season 4, Episode 6: "Chuck Versus the Aisle of Terror")

Big Mike adds that he is "not nearly scary enough to build a haunted house. You need to put some real crazies on that" – referring to Jeff and Lester – "if you want it done correctly."

After given the task of making the store fun and scary, Lester tells Jeff: "We got to tap into a place that is so scary, so demented, that it'll change Halloween as we know it. We got to tap into your head." Most of the store winds up being decorated in appropriately fun fashion, except for Jeffster's Aisle of Terror, which is just strange. As Morgan observes, "It's scary, but in a really bad way."

Chuck Business Tips

While episodes of *Chuck* make the point with humor, it's extremely frustrating to deal with employees who have little, if any, interest in doing their jobs, never mind the notion of more broadly looking for ways to make the firm more successful.

Unfortunately, there always seem to be workers who will find excuses to avoid pitching in when extra work must be done. Others rebel against almost any kind of authority.

For good measure, there is the question of employees who cannot be trusted to carry out tasks independently.

Business owners and managers cannot afford to simply assume that all employees possess the positive attitudes and motivations needed for business success. Quite simply, all workers do not have the same outlook regarding their jobs and the business as do the owners and managers.

To grasp this reality, contemplate the role of labor unions in business history. A union considers the well being of the business only if the firm's survival is in immediate jeopardy. Just take a look at the troubles of unionized auto manufacturers. The objective of labor unions is to maximize compensation for union members, while minimizing the amount of work needed to earn such compensation. While labor unions are nearly inconsequential in the private sector today – in 2010, only 6.9 percent of private sector workers were union members, compared to 24.2 percent in 1973, for example, according to Unionstats.com – labor union leanings or thinking among certain workers certainly has not completely evaporated.

Management must evaluate each employee, and gauge just how much oversight is required. This assessment is necessary not just to maintain or boost the productivity of a particular worker, but also to make sure that such an individual does not negatively affect other staff. After all, it is not necessary to take over and barricade the workplace to undermine management and a business. Indeed, undermining owners or managers is accomplished far more subtly, through complaining at desks or around the water cooler, for example. If left unchecked, those negatives can serve as a drain on an entire department or business.

Indeed, when employees go so far as to actively show that they have no real interest in work or the business, quick and decisive action by management is required. Otherwise, again, the department or business will suffer. Initial actions taken hopefully will be corrective, guiding the worker back on the right track. But if problems continue, then there must be increasingly severe responses, ranging from reprimands to suspensions to, if necessary, firing the worker.

"I couldn't give a rodent's behind about this job."

- Big Mike

4
The General Versus Big Mike: Who's the Boss?

Life is an ongoing learning experience, and that most certainly includes one's career.

Unfortunately, when gaining a management position, many people seem to forget this reality. Too many succumb to the fallacy that as the manager, they must know best, and therefore, have nothing to learn from others, including the people they are tasked to manage.

Others who gain management positions leave everyone else wondering how this advancement possibly occurred. They are clearly ill suited to guide and lead others.

And then there are those in business who view their promotion to manager as the time to take it easy, thinking of management as arriving on Easy Street.

All of the above, of course, are dead wrong. And falling into such thinking will only cut one's management career short.

At the Buy More, Big Mike serves as a conspicuous – though, again, quite amusing – example of a bad manager. Consider the following instances of Big Mike's misguided management principles:

• Big Mike tells Chuck that the best thing about being "Buy More brass" is "the medical." He then adds, "I couldn't give a rodent's behind about this job." (Season 1, Episode 6: "Chuck Versus the Sandworm")

• Referencing Big Mike to Lester and Jeff, Morgan says, "Gentlemen, I think that I speak for all of us when I say that the only reason that I took this job at the Buy More was to do as little work as humanly possible. And the big man, he made that dream a reality." Lester adds, "That man's an inspiration to slackers everywhere." (Season 2, Episode 13: "Chuck Versus the Suburbs")

• On the morning of Black Friday, with people banging on the doors of the Buy More, Big Mike offers the following speech to his employees: "Okay, listen up, in three minutes we let those animals in. If this was a zoo, I'd say run for your lives. But this is Buy More. For those days when you did squat, this is where you make up for it. Don't let me down. This is the single most important day of our year. And my door is locked. Don't even think about knocking." (Season 1, Episode 10: "Chuck Versus the Nemesis")

• After Lester, as assistant manager, fires all of the staff except for Chuck, the store is unmanned. Big Mike walks in, and fails to notice the lack of workers. He asks Lester, "And the managers-only doughnuts?" (Season 2, Episode 2: "Chuck Versus the Seduction")
Lester replies, "They're on your desk, sir."
And Big Mike is satisfied, declaring, "Tight ship you're running, Patel."

Meanwhile, in managing her CIA/NSA team, General Beckman presents a very different management philosophy. Consider the following examples:

• When it seems like a new Intersect will be ready, and Chuck is no longer needed, the General tells Casey: "We can't have another Intersect wandering around Los Angeles getting into trouble... You have your orders, Major. Tomorrow night, eliminate Chuck Bartowski." (Season 2, Episode 1: "Chuck Versus the First Date")

• During a critical juncture in the longtime pursuit of an objective, General Beckman feels that Chuck, Sarah and Casey have made costly errors. Concerned that matters could go further awry, she takes decisive action. Beckman directly takes over the operation. (Season 2, Episode 17: "Chuck Versus the Predator")

• At another point, the General recognizes that Chuck has done things that her regular agents have not been able to accomplish. Chuck doubts that he can be a spy. But the General tells him: "We are in the midst of a secret war with Fulcrum, and I believe the outcome of this fight will rest squarely on your shoulders." (Season 2, Episode 17: "Chuck Versus the Predator")
Chuck responds, "I'm no spy."
Beckman says, "Do you know how many agents I've lost to Fulcrum? How powerful they are? Only this operation, only you, have found a hole in their armor. See, I can't lose you, Chuck. I need you. It's time for you to become a spy."

• General Beckman is pleased with a mission plan from Chuck. She tells him: "I'm impressed. You've really progressed as a spy... You've put duty above emotion. I mean using Colonel Casey as bait? It usually takes years before an agent is willing to put his teammates in harm's way. Good tactical thinking, Bartowski." (Season 4, Episode 5: "Chuck Versus the Couch Lock")

• After promising that the government would do all it could to find and rescue Chuck's father (Scott Bakula), when the General discovers where Fulcrum is operating, she ignores that promise for national security purposes. When Casey asks if they are sending in a team to rescue Chuck's father, the General says, "We don't have time for that. I've ordered a squadron of F16s to annihilate the site." (Season 2, Episode 21: "Chuck Versus the Colonel")

Casey counters that he gave his word to Chuck that his father would be rescued.

Beckman declares, "I have not come to this decision lightly. We have no other choice."

• After Agent Daniel Shaw (Brandon Routh) finds out that Sarah, unknowingly, was the one who killed his wife a few years before, Chuck tells General Beckman: "The guy's got to be an emotional train wreck right now. Nobody can control their feelings that well." (Season 3, Episode 13: "Chuck Versus the Other Guy")

Beckman declares, "Chuck, what you are seeing in Shaw is an absolute professional. Something you are not."

It turns out, of course, that Chuck is right, and the General failed to see the risk.

Chuck Business Tips

It's hard to imagine two managers more different than Big Mike and General Beckman.

For example, Beckman stands willing to make the tough call or seize control of the situation when necessary. In contrast, Big Mike's gut tells him to avoid tough situations and hide in his office.

And while both Beckman and Big Mike recognize the need for their employees to succeed, Beckman sees that the growth of her employees will build the organization and help to meet the firm's mission. Big Mike only sees his own benefits. For example, Beckman compliments Chuck for his tactical thinking that advances the mission, while Big Mike gives a thumbs up to Lester for having the managers-only doughnuts ready, while the store is without workers.

In the end, Big Mike misses the fundamental point that managers lead by example. In his actions and declarations, Big Mike makes clear that he does not care about his job or the Buy More; is uninterested in hard work; and has no eye for detail in terms of what's going on in his store.

That being the case, should he expect anything more from his employees? Of course not. As Lester says, Big Mike serves as an inspiration to all slackers.

At the other end of the spectrum, Beckman is efficient, even ruthless, in her decision making, thereby setting an example for those who report to her.

Still even General Beckman has her management weaknesses. As noted in the example of her broken promise regarding Chuck's father, she can miss the importance of trust in an organization. As explored further in a later chapter, playing fast and loose with trust usually turns out to be very costly for a manager and a business.

In addition, Beckman proves to be a manager that struggles to get by her assumptions, as noted in her exchange with Chuck regarding the emotional state of Agent Shaw. Beckman was quick to dismiss Chuck's concerns due to her assumptions about Chuck being too emotional, and Shaw being the consummate professional spy no matter the circumstances.

Being limited by personal assumptions and experiences can prove fatal for a manger and a business.

Interestingly, there's a moment from *Chuck* when Beckman is willing to put aside all of her preconceptions about how to run things. Indeed, to achieve the organization's objectives, she is willing to go against nearly everything she has learned in terms of managing missions.

After the CIA/NSA takes over and runs the entire Buy More, Morgan sees a problem – the pace actually is *too* efficient and consumer friendly. Consider the following exchange between Morgan and the General as they stroll about the store. (Season 4, Episode 2: "Chuck Versus the Suitcase")

Morgan: "I'd like to talk to you about how well things are going here at the Buy More."

General: "Things do seem to be running quite smoothly."

Morgan: "Exactly, that seems to be the problem to me. It's too right that it's wrong."

General: "And tell me, Mr. Grimes, what do you know about running a CIA base?"

Morgan: "Nothing, but I do know how to run a Buy More, and with all due respect, General, this is no longer a Buy More."

General: "You have five minutes."

Morgan: "I only need two. Walk with me. You see, one of the defining characteristics of the old Buy More was its inattention to detail..."

General: "My people were trained to be observant and efficient. It's the CIA way."

Morgan: "Aah, but it's not the Buy More way, you see. Now if customers don't have hazardous spills, mislabeled products, surly employees to distract them, well, they might start to enjoy their time here... You have to look at the big picture here. A pleased customer is going to want to stay in the store longer. He's going to want to bring his friends, maybe bring his family, tying up valuable CIA resources, not to mention encouraging them to look a little deeper. And what happens, General, what happens when they do look a little deeper? Maybe, maybe, just one customer discovers what's really going on here... General, look, if even I can see through this Buy More cover, what's an enemy spy going to think?"

Morgan recognizes what's needed to run a successful establishment. But he also sees that this is not what's needed to meet the CIA's goals and objectives. His solution is to rehire the incompetents that previously worked at the Buy More.

The lesson here is not to hire poor workers. Instead, it's that managers often have to be willing to think completely outside the box to get the job done. In rare circumstances, being a good manager might require putting aside all you have learned about managing a business, and going in an entirely different direction. That requires vision on the part of a manager.

"Yesterday, I was making eleven bucks an hour fixing computers, now I have one in my brain."

- Chuck

5
Chuck Versus Chuck: Which Chuck Are You?

What are you experiencing in terms of your career – growth, stagnation, bewilderment, or frustration?

Particularly over the first two seasons of the television series, Chuck Bartowski had a tough time figuring out what he wanted to do with his life. He felt stuck in a dead end job at the Buy More's Nerd Herd. At the same time, he wanted the Intersect, the CIA, and NSA out of his life.

It's not unusual for people to feel a bit lost at various times in their careers. It's pretty typical, for example, to get frustrated with the boss, co-workers, or a lack of advancement. Others discover that they just want to do something completely different, but might be afraid or unable to make the big jump. The worst case occurs when feeling stuck in a job you hate. It can take a toll on the individual.

There also is the case of family, friends or colleagues believing that they know better what you should be doing.

Of course, it's a good idea to seek advice from trusted sources, such as a mentor. But even in these cases, guidance needs to be weighed and put in proper perspective. For example, as a college professor, I occasionally am asked for career advice. My responses always are twofold.

First, I note that all of the career advice I received in college from professors was bad – and I mean really bad. Second, my bottom line suggestion is to do what you are going to enjoy. We spend an enormous chunk of our lives working, and spending all that time in a job you hate makes for a fairly miserable existence. It's also likely that you'll eventually wind up doing the bare minimum to get by.

Consider a few snippets on the lost and frustrated Chuck when it comes to his career:

• As noted earlier, after the Intersect is inserted in Chuck's head, he points out, "Yesterday, I was making eleven bucks an hour fixing computers, now I have one in my brain." Chuck is bewildered. (Season 1, Episode 1: "Chuck: The Pilot")

• During an early episode in Chuck's story, the focus was on his future. (Season 1, Episode 3: "Chuck Versus the Tango")

Big Mike asks Chuck: "Bartowski, what is it that you want out of life? ... We're talking Buy More – career objectives. Where do you see yourself in five years, ten years?"

Chuck responds, "I have absolutely no idea."

A bit later, while Chuck is reading an issue of *PC Gamer*, Morgan and Ellie are debating where Chuck is and should go. Morgan says Chuck's too fragile to leave the Buy More, while Ellie counters that Chuck is beyond the Buy More. Meanwhile, Chuck has either tuned them out or simply does not care.

But we see his frustration when Sarah mentions that Chuck needs a cover identity for their mission. He offers the name Charles Carmichael, and presents a rather detailed description of who that is: "Graduated with honors from Stanford. Runs a hugely successful software company. Semi-retired and is considering entering America's Cup." That's where Chuck envisioned his life heading before being detoured.

Finally, Chuck admits to Ellie that he wants to finish college, travel, and "learn an obscure language that only really cool people know." And he notes that "not one of my dreams involves working at the Buy More for another week." But by the end of the episode, due to still being the only Intersect, that's exactly where Chuck finds himself – feeling trapped in the Buy More.

Eventually, though, things start to move in a positive direction for Chuck:

• A key moment that derailed Chuck's career dreams occurred when he was kicked out of Stanford for allegedly stealing exams (which he did not do), leaving him 12 credits short of his degree. However, after some time as the Intersect, Sarah and Casey make sure that Chuck's fieldwork with the CIA earns his degree from Stanford. (Season 2, Episode 5: "Chuck Versus Tom Sawyer")

• When his old college friend Bryce dies at the hands of evil agents, Chuck summons the courage to download the Intersect into his brain, destroy the computer so the Ring organization does not gain access, and save Casey and Sarah with his new combat skills. (Season 2, Episode 22: "Chuck Versus the Ring")

• With Los Angeles threatened by a ticking suitcase nuke, the two Intersect agents sent to replace Chuck have no idea what to do. But Chuck figures out that the bomb can be deactivated with salt water, so he winds up using the contents of his juice box to get the job done. (Season 4, Episode 19: "Chuck Versus the Muuurder")

Chuck Business Tips

Chuck quite easily could have given up when faced with setbacks and various frustrations, or decided that new opportunities would not work out and therefore were not even worth trying.

But after a brief time of being lost and feeling discouraged, Chuck decides to seize the day. He, in fact, wants to be a spy, and works to prove himself to the people who matter. Chuck not only chooses to take advantage of the Intersect being placed in his head, but also creates his own opportunities for success through courage and ingenuity.

In the end, career success and satisfaction depend upon creating opportunities and deciding what to do with the opportunities that come your way.

That requires (unlike Chuck) some degree of managing your own career. Ideally, a career plan should be developed that identifies goals; offers an action plan on how to reach those goals; and allows for flexibility with new challenges and opportunities.

Peter F. Drucker, who was a leading management teacher and consultant, wrote, "Most of us ... have to learn to manage ourselves." In an essay titled "Managing Oneself" (from *The Essentials: An Introduction to the Most Enduring Ideas on Management from Harvard Business Review*, Harvard Business Review Press, Boston, 2011), Drucker laid out a five-step process for this self-management: 1) identifying and building up strengths while remedying bad habits; 2) figuring out how and when you best perform, such as being a listener or reader, loner or team member, and decision maker or adviser; 3) assessing personal values and what kind of organization they align with; 4) determining where you belong; and finally, 5) figuring out what one should contribute and achieve.

In the midst of this self-management process, beyond issues like education, training, financing and networking, it must be understood what traits – such as hard work, persistence, discipline, ingenuity, and personal integrity – will be required to meet career goals.

Chuck wound up achieving success, and that was, in part, due to his skills and eventual willingness to capitalize on opportunity. However, there obviously was a great deal of happenstance involved as well, with Chuck simply falling into situations. Though it's hard to envision being tossed into the life of a spy from working at an electronics store, Chuck still could have used a career plan.

"I hotwired the control panel using my stupid pocket protector, thank you very much."

\- Chuck

6

Chuck Versus The Intersect: Is Technology Your Friend or Foe?

Is technology your friend or foe?

Oh, come on, how could that question even be asked? After all, this is the twenty-first century. It's obvious that technology has been a boon to businesses.

Just consider how computer, Internet, digital, broadband and wireless technologies have transformed daily enterprise in recent times. While all types of firms have reaped big rewards, small businesses arguably have benefited most. Quite simply, a small business today can reach potential customers across the nation and around the globe, when not that long ago they might have been limited to local or regional markets. The number of home-based businesses has exploded, and both owners and employees have become more mobile.

Technology also means that tremendous efficiencies and cost savings can be achieved, including increased and immediate access to large amounts of information, an expanded universe of individuals and businesses to contract or partner with, and making regular work duties, from writing and sending letters to tracking product quality and worker performance measures, far more efficient.

Technology plays a big part in Chuck's life. He works in the Nerd Herd at the Buy More (again, think the Geek Squad at Best Buy) repairing and installing assorted electronics. For good measure, he is an avid gamer.

At the same time, however, Chuck initially felt like his life was ruined by the Intersect. He wanted the Intersect out of his head, feeling overwhelmed, manipulated and trapped by this technology.

Eventually, though, Chuck grows to see that the Intersect will help change his life for the better, allowing him to break free from the Buy More to become an international spy.

Chuck Business Tips

Consider four cases from *Chuck* that reflect potential questions and benefits that come with technology.

• Jeff and Lester go to Big Mike with a request to go to a technology expo where a new operating system is to be introduced. (Season 2, Episode 19: "Chuck Versus the Dream Job")

Lester declares, "We believe that attending that release will make us better employees."

With Jeff adding, "And better human beings."

Big Mikes responds, "Good thinking. Send Bartowski."

When Jeff and Lester say Chuck is not here, Big Mike says, "Okay fine. You both can go. Have fun camping out at the weirdo convention."

This situation raises the issue of whether technology is being used to boost productivity, or simply serve as a vehicle for goofing off by employees. Let's face reality, Internet sites, e-mail, texting, Facebook, and Twitter, for example, not only benefit businesses, but also can distract employees from their work tasks.

Just consider the productivity lost when Google put a playable version of Pac-Man on its homepage. In a May 25, 2010, Cnet.com column ("Study: Pac-Man on Google wasted 4.8 million hours"), Daniel Terdiman reported:

> According to a study by RescueTime, Pac-Man on Google – the playable version of the iconic game that the search giant replaced its home page logo with on Friday – cost the economy a total of 4,819,352 man-hours and a whopping $120,483,800 in lost productivity. As RescueTime put it, you could hire every single Google employee, including co-founders Larry Page, Sergey Brin, and CEO Eric Schmidt, and get them for six weeks for that much money.

Managers must be aware of the possibility of lost time to online escapades, while also recognizing that these technologies are deeply ingrained in many people's lives today. Taking all of this into account, the manager must create a balanced policy that keeps the focus on work, but also does not cross over the line to make personnel feel like children and that they are not trusted. That's not always an easy balance to strike.

• Chuck's father creates a program to get the Intersect out of Chuck's head. Once that happens, Chuck says he feels "lighter," and seems both relieved and pleased. (Season 2, Episode 21: "Chuck Versus the Colonel")

However, in the very next episode, Chuck downloads a new Intersect in order to become the hero who will save Sarah and Casey, stop the evil Ring, and set him on a path of seeking to become a real spy. (Season 2, Episode 22: "Chuck Versus the Ring")

This is a transformative moment when Chuck shifts from viewing the Intersect as a burden to accepting it as a means for growth and opportunity. Many businesses and managers must go through this kind of transformation. New technologies initially can be seen as burdens, adding to capital and training costs. But eventually, if all is done according to a sound plan, the benefits of investments in technology should become apparent to all.

• Director Bentley (Robin Givens) looks down on Chuck and his "stupid pocket protector." Could this be taken as an example of a co-worker having an anti-technology streak? Later, Chuck uses the tools in that pocket protector to save her life. He tells Bentley: "I hotwired the control panel using my stupid pocket protector, thank you very much." (Season 4, Episode 19: "Chuck Versus the Muuurder")

A manager will have to deal with some employees who are not just reluctant, but downright hostile to technology in general, and in particular, to technological change. Chuck won over Director Bentley by saving her life, but for most managers, it's not so drastic. But it is critical that they communicate and illustrate clearly how technology will benefit each worker and the firm overall.

• After the Intersect is forcibly taken, Chuck now feels that he cannot save Sarah without it. But Casey tells him: "Shut up. You're Chuck Bartowski, the second-best spy I ever worked with. Now, you're going to go save the best." (Season 4, Episode 24: "Chuck Versus the Cliffhanger")

This is the difference between technology empowering individuals as opposed to serving as an artificial crutch.

Are the skills and abilities of managers and employees broadened, enhanced and strengthened by technology, or are they actually narrowed, limited and, in a sense, dumbed down to be able to accomplish only what the technology allows them to do?

Technology truly helps to build Chuck up. As a manager, are you making sure that's the case for you, your employees and your business? In the end, a business needs to develop a strategy for information technology. Within the context the firm's mission, goals and plan, it must be assessed how technology fits in to achieve success.

"... the most important thing about leadership is to convince everybody that you have everything under control."

- Sarah

7

Chuck Versus Leadership? Leading To Get Things Done

What makes a good leader in business? Considering the many different management styles of very successful business leaders over the years, that's not an easy question to answer.

Leadership has become a hot topic in business schools. Indeed, many schools now offer MBA degrees in leadership. However, debate still rages over whether or not leadership can be taught. In the end, parts of being a good leader can be taught – such as in the areas of decision-making and motivating employees – while other aspects of leadership turn out to be more innate and intangible.

While the *Chuck* television series excels at showing what *not* to do in business, on this issue of leadership, it provides a powerful, positive lesson.

• After Chuck and his Nerd Herd team get the job done repairing a bunch of computers, Big Mike tells Chuck, "I'm impressed, and I'm not a man easily impressed." (Season 1, Episode 3: "Chuck Versus the Tango")

Chuck replies, "I think you should know that I only fixed the last few. My team did most of the work. They deserve the credit. And you're only as good as your team."

Big Mike's response? "First rule of management: Always take the credit."

• General Beckman puts Chuck in the leadership position overseeing all aspects of the Intersect project. His first responsibility is to find new Intersect candidates similar to himself. As his project comes under fire and is unraveling, Chuck is worried and unsure. (Season 4, Episode 19: "Chuck Versus the Muuurder")

Sarah advises, "You are still in charge. You need to be calm and confident." And a bit later, she continues, "Listen, Chuck, the most important thing about leadership is to convince everybody that you have everything under control... Chuck, you're not in charge by accident. You did disarm a nuclear bomb using fruit juice. Okay, you can do this. We're right behind you."

Later, when a bomb threatens all, Director Bentley takes the explosive into a room that can contain the blast. But it can only be closed manually from the inside. She is willing to sacrifice herself for the others. She tells Chuck, "This is what a leader does."

But Chuck is able to save her as well, by using his techie skills to hotwire the room's control panel.

At the end of the mission, the General tells Chuck, "You are a true leader."

Chuck replies, "Thank you, General, but I'm only as strong as the team that surrounds me, and as always, Sarah and Casey were my eyes, ears and more today." Later, Chuck notes, "General, if I could just add something quickly? Director Bentley was invaluable today."

Chuck Business Tips

Leadership is not just about getting people to follow you, but to stir them to do so enthusiastically. Specifically as a manager, leadership is about guiding, inspiring and motivating employees to subscribe to the firm's mission, and pursue and achieve its goals and objectives.

Big Mike, by declaring that a manager should simply take credit for what gets done, shows that he is not a leader, and that employees have little reason to follow him.

In contrast, Chuck exhibits true leadership by stressing the importance of his team, and giving credit to those who perform well. He makes this clear with his Nerd Herd team in the first case above, and with Sarah, Casey, and Director Bentley in the second instance.

Chuck also understands the idea of leading by example. He builds confidence in those he works with by showing how to achieve the objective. In the case of shielding the effects of a bomb blast, he finds a way to get it done without anyone being hurt or dying.

Sarah hits on a fundamental issue on leadership when declaring that "the most important thing about leadership is to convince everybody that you have everything under control." Business is littered with organizations that suffered due to the person at the top losing control, failing to lay out a clear mission and goals, not making decisions, and not having a clue as to how to motivate and guide staff in the right direction.

Over the years, I've had the good fortune of working for several excellent leaders. A few, for example, excelled at motivating their team, and shared credit for accomplishments in an honest and appropriate manner – like Chuck. Another did a fine job at leading by example. One manager performed well by motivating the team, and getting them to work well together.

On the flip side, I've fortunately never worked with someone who selfishly grabbed all the credit for achievements. But there have been managers who didn't have a clue as to the leadership aspects of their position.

One failed to understand that employees tend to hang on every word a manager utters, and pay extremely close attention to a manager's actions. Another manager clearly lacked the experience, depth, knowledge and communication skills needed to lead, and the result was a quick loss of respect for the manager and a decline in the organization. This manager failed the basic Sarah test of leadership, i.e., the person failed to convince anyone that anything was under control.

Leadership is more than just managing people and the organization well. Leadership, again, is about inspiring people to believe in what the firm is doing, and encouraging them to use their talents, skills, creativity and energies to take the business into the realm of greatness.

What kinds of traits are needed to be a leader in business? Clearly, leaders must be optimistic (can you imagine being inspired by a pessimist?), confident (Chuck came close to losing the ability to lead when he was worried and unsure), decisive (ever heard of a great, indecisive leader?), of high character and trustworthy (who is inspired to follow someone they cannot trust to do what's right?), an excellent communicator, and able to understand and tap into the strengths of their employees.

Again, the question is: While understanding the traits and requirements of leadership, how much of it can be taught and how much is the result of who the person is?

"You're slightly unmotivated, a bit of an underachiever, but a loser? That's not your turf."

- Morgan

8

Chuck Versus the Cheeseballs: Dealing with Failure

Failure sucks. Nonetheless, failure is part of life, and it's certainly part of business. It also can be a valuable experience for learning important lessons.

Many entrepreneurs, for example, experience business failure – sometimes multiple failures – before they hit on the idea, the right enterprise, that succeeds. But even successful firms will undertake ventures that ultimately come up short.

It's not all that different on the career front. For most of us, the career path is not a smooth ride relentlessly higher. Instead, there tend to be some potholes, detours or roadblocks along the way.

The question is: What do business owners, managers and individuals do with failure?

Consider two *Chuck* examples.

• In 1983, after dedicating three years of his life to a video game, Jeff was the Missile Command world champion. He was on top of his world, with the media and beautiful women seeking him out. (Season 1, Episode 5: "Chuck Versus Tom Sawyer")

But success was fleeting. Later, after decades of drinking, drugs and who knows what else, Jeff has the opportunity to return to greatness – to reach the kill screen of Missile Command. But he faints in front of cheering fans before even beginning his return.

Later, after Chuck beats the game, Jeff goes back to playing Missile Command, but with no one else around.

• After choosing to not run away with Sarah, Chuck fails the training to become a real spy. He has lost everything he wanted – Sarah, the "girl of his dreams," and the life of a spy. (Season 3, Episode 1: "Chuck Versus the Pink Slip")

What does Chuck do?

Initially, he sleeps, sits on the couch in a bathrobe, watches television, lets his facial hair grow, and eats cheese balls. The only thing that motivates him to get off the couch is to get more cheese balls at the Buy More.

After Chuck is recognized despite his disguise of dark sunglasses, hat, beard and robe, Emmett says Chuck carries the "putrid stench of failure," telling others "that's why you don't leave the Buy More." He adds to Chuck: "My God, you're pathetic."

Later, Morgan attempts some encouragement by telling Chuck: "You're slightly unmotivated, a bit of an underachiever, but a loser? That's not your turf."

Chuck responds, "I blew it buddy, opportunity of a lifetime. Without getting into specifics, I had a job offer that would have included a lot of travel and excitement, and I've already been fired from it twice."

But Chuck eventually decides to get back in the game, to prove that he indeed can be a good spy.

Chuck Business Tips

Failure crushes Jeff, with the life squeezed out of him. In contrast, after suffering setbacks and briefly wallowing in some self-pity, Chuck rises above his failure.

The fundamental difference is that Chuck learns and ultimately grows due to his failure.

In one's career and in business in general, failure must be treated as a learning opportunity. If not, it has the ability to make one bitter, pessimistic, and stagnant. It's not unusual to try to shift the blame to others for one's own mistakes or shortcomings.

As noted earlier, most successful entrepreneurs have experienced failure, learned from such setbacks, and ultimately treated failure as temporary stops while climbing the ladder of success.

Examples include Milton Hershey, who failed several times in the candy business, before founding and building the Hershey Company. And even after establishing this market-leading chocolate candy manufacturer, there were some failures along the way, including chewing gum and a bad bet borrowing in the sugar market.

Steve Jobs, co-founder of Apple Inc, who was either ousted from or chose to leave the firm in 1985, failed at his new venture Next. But in 1997, Jobs returned to lead an Apple that was on the brink of bankruptcy, subsequently taking the company to a global technology leader.

In an October 2, 2010, *New York Times* article titled "What Steve Jobs Learned in the Wilderness," Randall Stross, a professor at San Jose State University, pointed out:

> The Steve Jobs who returned to Apple was a much more capable leader — precisely because he had been badly banged up. He had spent 12 tumultuous, painful years failing to find a way to

make the new company profitable... And he had always been able to attract great talent. What he hadn't learned before returning to Apple, however, was the necessity of retaining it. He has now done so. One of the unremarked aspects of Apple's recent story is the stability of the executive team — no curb filled with dumped managers. Kevin Compton, who was a senior executive at Businessland during the Next years, described Mr. Jobs after returning to Apple: "He's the same Steve in his passion for excellence, but a new Steve in his understanding of how to empower a large company to realize his vision." Mr. Jobs had learned from Next not to try to do everything himself, Mr. Compton said.

An amusing *Chuck* moment highlights the lofty position Apple has risen to in recent years. Lester tells Chuck that the Nerd Herd has a Linux install.

Chuck asks, "I'm sorry, why can't you and Jeff go?"

Lester laughs in a mocking tone, and says, "Linux, PCs, we're Mac guys, Chuck. We're IT artists." (Season 1, Episode 2: "Chuck Versus the Helicopter")

The lofty success achieved by Jobs at Apple was unlikely without Steve Jobs having experienced and learned from his failures.

Managers need to keep in mind the idea of failure as a teaching moment when dealing with their employees. Failure is going to occur to some degree in any organization. Managers need to not only communicate clearly the consequences or costs of failure, but also provide feedback so that workers can learn from failure and over the longer haul, become better employees and more successful individuals.

*"Sometimes your dream job isn't always
what you expect it to be."*

\- Chuck

9
Chuck Versus
the Not-So-Dream Job?
What is the Dream Job?

Consider a real-life case of getting and losing the dream job.

Early in his career, in a span of about five months, this person left a comfortable career for a dream job with a leading individual in a different industry, but wound up being unemployed looking for a new position. It was one of those moments that can affect a career over the long haul for better or worse.

This industry leader excelled at providing a particular service. Unfortunately, just because someone performs well in certain areas does not necessarily mean that he communicates well with and adequately manages others.

The dream job turned into the career nightmare of being unemployed.

As Chuck admits when confronted by Casey with a threat to keep his mouth shut regarding some rogue action, "Sometimes your dream job isn't always what you expect it to be." (Season 3, Episode 10: "Chuck Versus the Tic Tac")

Also consider the following regarding the dream job:

• Chuck is sent in undercover at a computer software firm, Roark Instruments, that he dreamed of working for since college. He gets the job, and is excited. (Season 2, Episode 19: "Chuck Versus the Dream Job")

Chuck tells Sarah: "It's weird. Even though I know it's not real, I am excited about this job... If I had gotten this job at Roark right after college, maybe I never become the Intersect. Then when my dad comes back after ten years, I can show him that I'm not just another loser working at a Buy More."

• Morgan has always dreamed of being a Benihana chef in Hawaii. He finally stands up to the abuse doled out by store manager Emmett, and quits to pursue his dream job. He leaves the Buy More to applause, and Lester yelling, "You're free, Morgan." (Season 2, Episode 21: "Chuck Versus the Colonel")

Unfortunately, he later returns from Hawaii because he "couldn't flip the shrimp." (Season 3, Episode 1: "Chuck Versus the Pink Slip")

Chuck Business Tips

Is the dream job simply too good to be true?

In the two examples above, things did not work out for Chuck or Morgan. Chuck wonders what might have been if he had landed the software position earlier in his career, and as a real job rather than a spy cover. Meanwhile, Morgan takes a chance to pursue his dream job, but then falls back to earth.

The dream job, though, does not have to be unachievable or too good to be true. But when it comes to your career, dreams must be firmly rooted in reality. While work and career should be enjoyable, it is not going to be completely free from any strife or problems. Life does not work that way. All human endeavors have some flaws – to varying degrees.

The dream job should not be romanticized. While that job is out there for the taking, there can be costs involved.

One of the oddest cases of dream job costs came in pure dollar terms. It was widely reported in September 2011 that Ted Weschler landed his dream job to make some of the investment decisions for Warren Buffett's Berkshire Hathaway.

Writing for *Fortune* magazine ("Meet Ted Weschler: Buffett auction winner, Berkshire's new hire," September 12, 2011), Carol Loomis explains that Weschler, a successful hedge fund manager, as part of a charity auction, won a private lunch with Buffett in 2010, and won the auction again in 2011. Weschler donated a staggering $2,626,311 in 2010 and another $2,626,411 in 2011 for the privilege. The result? Loomis notes: "Buffett almost apologetically sounded out Weschler about the possibility of his joining Berkshire. 'I very much wanted him to do it, but I didn't expect to get very far with the idea,' Buffett told Fortune. 'Ted will no doubt make a lot of money at Berkshire. But he was already making a lot of money with his fund – you can get an idea of that from the size of his Glide bids – so money wasn't a reason for him to come.' Even so, Weschler said right away he'd think it over – and within weeks came to the conclusion that he wanted to accept Buffett's offer."

Few people can spend $5,252,722 to, in effect, land their dream job. But the point that seeking out and finding that position, as well as continuing in the dream job, has costs is important to keep in mind. Of course, other kinds of costs, beyond straight dollars and cents, come into play.

At a crucial point, Chuck must make a difficult choice – the dream job of travel and excitement as a spy, or leaving it all behind to run away with Sarah. Later, explaining his decision to Sarah to choose the spy life, Chuck says,

"Sarah, they wanted me to be a spy, okay. They told me that I could make a difference. For years, I've been kicking around, not knowing what I wanted to do with my life, like a loser. And then one day, really important people told me that they thought I could change the world, me, Chuck Bartowski." (Season 3, Episode 1: "Chuck Versus the Pink Slip")

That's a dream job moment. And while Chuck suffers some temporary setbacks, he does in fact go on to do important things and make a real difference in people's lives. He accomplishes this by coming to better understand his strengths, learning from those around him, managing to see and capitalize on opportunities, and putting work, including the dream job, in proper perspective. More on that last point in a later chapter, but it's worth highlighting that Chuck eventually does get the dream girl and the dream job.

"Insurgents. I hate insurgents."

- Casey

10
John Casey Versus Daniel Shaw: Company Man Versus Company Turncoat

There are individuals who truly have the best interests of the company in mind. But other individuals can appear that way, but have a very different agenda. Managers must be able to discern between the company man, if you will, and the potential company turncoat.

Indeed, based on the following examples, could there by anyone out there that is more of a company man than John Casey?

• With a new Intersect being readied, Chuck is no longer needed. The General orders Casey to eliminate Chuck, noting, "We can't have another Intersect wandering around Los Angeles getting into trouble." (Season 2, Episode 1: "Chuck Versus the First Date")

Casey clearly is reluctant. At one point, he tells the General: "Chuck served his country with honor, maybe he even has potential as an analyst for the organization." But when the order stands, he seems willing to carry out his orders despite his personal feelings. Fortunately, the final choice to pull or not pull the trigger becomes unnecessary.

• As assistant manager, Morgan asks Casey for his help to regain control of the Buy More. Morgan says to Casey: "I need you. Okay, please help me. I don't know what they'll do next. Lester and his gang, they've taken over the store. They set booby traps for me everywhere. I'm going crazy here. I can't fight them by myself anymore. They don't follow any rules." (Season 3, Episode 5: "Chuck Versus First Class")

Casey responds, "Insurgents. I hate insurgents."

Morgan says, "Then this will work out, I think."

Later, Casey kidnaps and brainwashes Lester.

Subsequently, when Jeff asks what they are going to do about Morgan, Lester, straight out of *The Manchurian Candidate*, says, "Morgan Grimes is the kindest, warmest, most understanding human being I have ever known in my life."

Seeing this, Morgan tells Casey: "Wow, that is too cool. How did you do that?"

Casey advises, "Don't ask. Plausible deniability."

• Casey is shot and temporarily limited to a wheelchair. Nonetheless, he is willing to risk his life, and go on a mission for his country. Declaring his readiness to go to Costa Gravas, Casey says, "I know every corner of the godforsaken slime hole." (Season 4, Episode 4: "Chuck Versus the Coup d'Etat")

• During a flashback to 1999, Casey's team is in Iran, under orders to secure a gold reserve so it cannot be used to fund terrorists. However, the rest of his team wants the gold for themselves. (Season 4, Episode 5: "Chuck Versus the Couch Lock")

Regarding the mission, at one point Casey says, "We are under strict orders from President Clinton to seal this place up. While I might not like him, or his mouthy wife, those are the orders."

When his team turns on him, Casey beats them single-handedly and drags them across the desert to prison.

• Make no mistake, Casey truly loves his work. When heading off to Las Vegas for Chuck's bachelor party, Casey talks up the city's gun ranges, noting, "I brought some of my fancy targets," namely, one with Osama bin Laden. (Season 4, Episode 22: "Chuck Versus Agent X")

Then there is Agent Daniel Shaw, who seems to be a super spy, the perfect professional and willing to do anything to stop the evil Ring. But when he finds out that Sarah is the one who killed his wife (under orders), Shaw turns on the CIA and his nation. (Season 3, Episode 12: "Chuck Versus the American Hero")

Chuck discovers that Shaw is a traitor, and is going to kill Sarah. Chuck and Morgan fittingly go to Casey for help. Chuck tells Casey: "You're the ultimate spy." (Season 3, Episode 13: "Chuck Versus the Other Guy")

With the help of Casey and Morgan, Chuck takes down Shaw. Casey, with the Ring director in his custody, agrees to make a deal with the General. All he wants after being fired from the NSA is full reinstatement at his old rank, along with a new Crown Victoria and the addition of Morgan as a member of Team Bartowski.

Chuck Business Tips

When news of a business scandal – or spy scandal, for that matter – breaks, it's not unusual for the co-workers of the wrongdoer to express how shocked they are, that they never expected that this person was capable of doing such things.

But it is part of a good criminal's job to not look suspicious.

This puts managers in a difficult position. You have to trust your employees, while also making sure that no one does anything wrong, and react quickly and appropriate to wrongdoing. In the end, it's all about establishing a system of ethics in the firm that apply to all. To quote John Casey's favorite president, Ronald Reagan, "Trust but verify."

Many businesses create a code of ethics that provides ethical expectations for all who work there, including explaining the firm's values, emphasizing the importance of integrity and respecting others, and making clear the importance of following policy and procedures, and abiding by all laws. In addition, there is little downside to offering specifics on unethical behavior and the consequences for such actions, including being fired. Employees at a firm often must sign any code of ethics, so no doubts or confusion exist.

But a code of ethics needs to be reinforced by action. That means owners and managers must make sound ethics part of the firm's culture, including showing that each person – both the worker and the customer – is treated with honestly and integrity. It's best when the Golden Rule reigns, i.e., do unto others as you would have them do unto you.

Why bother with anything along the lines of a code of ethics? After all, can you really imagine your most trusted employee or co-worker stealing or spying? Probably not, but that's the scenario Daniel Shaw presents. Indeed, could circumstances exist where even Casey might turn?

Consider the following case:

• In 1989, Casey was given the choice of serving his country with a secret black ops group, but if so, leaving his family behind. Years later, his former black ops boss, who was dishonorably discharged and had gone rogue, asks Casey to steal a pill that suppresses emotion from the CIA. After mistakenly being revealed by Chuck – who sees this as a test because he cannot believe that Casey would do anything to hurt his country – Casey is arrested for treason. It turns out that Casey must deliver the pill to the Ring in order to save his former fiancée, who will be killed if he does not deliver. (Season 3, Episode 10: "Casey Versus the Tic Tac")

Does this mean anyone can go over to the dark side? No. It simply means that John Casey would only take such an action to protect an innocent loved one. Hey, this is John Casey that we're talking about here.

"Is there anybody you haven't told about our fight?"

- Sarah

11
Chuck Versus Communication: Communicating in the Workplace

Relationships, whether of the personal or business varieties, can suffer enormously due to a lack of communication.

It's amazing, though, how many managers fail to communicate clearly and regularly with their employees. But it's often hard to figure out whether some managers deem it unnecessary to communicate, or if they are simply poor communicators. In addition, the ills of weak communication become glaringly apparent to all in the business, particularly those reporting to the manager, except for the uncommunicative manager.

The following examples from *Chuck* are a bit more realistic than they should be for a television comedy spy show.

• When Chuck is upset about the make up of Team Bartowski, he asks, "General, if I could speak freely." (Season 3, Episode 13: "Chuck Versus the Other Guy")

She responds, "That's not a good idea."

• Regarding the inability of Chuck and Sarah to communicate adequately, Morgan says sarcastically to Chuck: "You both are crack communicators." Morgan suggests a book: *101 Conversations Before "I Do"* by Dr. Fred. Chuck, without revealing the title to Sarah, brings up various questions raised in the book, working on their communications exercises, during a mission. (Season 4, Episode 4: "Chuck Versus the Coup d'Etat")

• After Chuck and Sarah have their first fight, Chuck winds up talking to everyone about it, including someone he does not even know, except Sarah. (Season 4, Episode 7: "Chuck Versus the First Fight")

That, of course, further aggravates Sarah. She asks, "Is there anybody you haven't told about our fight?... I can't believe you talked to everybody about our fight except for me." Meanwhile, Sarah talks to no one about the spat.

Chuck Business Tips

These three instances offer grains of truth for the real world on what not to do regarding communications.

General Beckman shoots down the idea of having her employee speak freely about the work situation. As a general policy, actual or implied, that's not only a surefire recipe for creating frustrations and resentment, but also means that the manager is bound to miss important developments in the workplace.

In the second case, Chuck does not have a bad idea in trying to get some guidance on how to improve communications. However, his strategy of trying to improve communications without being honest about how he is doing it not only is ironic, but also threatens to undercut the entire effort. And that turns out to be the eventual result.

In the last example, Chuck makes the mistake of communicating with everyone except for the person that matters. Not only is that also ironic, but at minimum, it accomplishes nothing, and at worst, it creates more trouble.

A manager not only should have official lines of communication established about what's going on in the department and business, but also should set up more informal channels of communication, making clear to co-workers and staff that all kinds of constructive communication, including feedback and questions, are welcome. That can be invaluable for the business.

At the same time, communication must be clear and straightforward. When managers are bad communicators, bad things happen in the business. Confusion mounts. Frustrations grow. Respect is lost. Other forms of communication, like gossip and complaints, fill the void left by management's inability to communicate properly.

Clear and straightforward communication is comprehensive (leaving no room for misinterpretation), constructive (whether it be offering praise, relaying important information or presenting solutions to problems), honest, respectful, firmly rooted in the facts, open to feedback, and free from sloppy errors.

In an era in which so many avenues of communication exist, and both employees and customers have expectations for increased communications, business owners or managers have to establish and execute sound, comprehensive communications policies.

"Okay, but you better be fine, or else I'll really kill you."

- Sarah

12
Casey Versus Sarah? Developing a Partnership

For several years, I co-wrote a newspaper column with a partner. Carolan & Keating ran for several years in *Newsday* on Long Island.

People always used to ask, "How do you write a column every week with another person?" For Matt Carolan and myself, it was pretty smooth sailing. That was due to three aspects of our partnership.

First, we held the same views 98 percent of the time on the various topics. That makes it a heck of a lot easier to write a commentary column.

Second, we had a system that worked. We would lay out the basics of what we wanted to say each week; one person would take the lead by writing the first draft; and then we'd go back and forth a bit to arrive at the final product. Even this explanation sounds more cumbersome than the process actually was.

And that was largely due to the third, and arguably most crucial aspect of our partnership: we had been good friends since high school, and trusted each other. There was no need to go through the fits and starts that many partnerships have to deal with as they move forward.

Quite frankly, we were lucky. When it comes to starting up and running a business, it seems like much of the advice on partnerships is the following: Only do it as a last resort.

The relationship between the CIA's Sarah Walker and the NSA's John Casey came a long way over the first four seasons of *Chuck*.

• When they start working together, trust is completely absent in the relationship between Casey and Sarah. In fact, Casey tells Chuck that he should not trust Sarah, and Sarah tells Chuck the same about Casey. This even leads to Casey and Sarah having a full-blown fight in the Wienerlicious (Sarah's cover job). (Season 1, Episode 2: "Chuck Versus the Helicopter")

• However, Sarah and Casey do start the process of working together. For example, Casey saves Sarah from enemy agents, and together they save Chuck and catch one of the world's most elusive arms dealers. (Season 1, Episode 3: "Chuck Versus the Tango")

• As more time passes, when another agent criticizes Sarah, Casey declares, "Walker, she's a pro. Not only that, she's the best damn partner I ever had." (Season 2, Episode 18: "Chuck Versus the Broken Heart")

• By the end of the second season of *Chuck*, Casey not only covers for Sarah with the General, but also gives her full credit for a successful mission. (Season 2, Episode 21: "Chuck Versus the Colonel")

General Beckman says, "Colonel Casey, am I to understand that you rescued Mr. Bartowski, recovered the Intersect cube, and destroyed Fulcrum's operation base?"

Casey responds, "That's correct."

The General adds, "Perhaps I should be promoting you to General?"

Casey points out, "Actually, Agent Walker's the one responsible for the success of the mission. She pretended to go AWOL, used herself and the asset as bait to lure Fulcrum out so we could secure their location. She risked her life to preserve the integrity of the mission. If anyone deserves a commendation, it's Walker."

• Later, the evil Alexi Volkoff (Timothy Dalton) directs Sarah to kill Casey in order to prove that she has left the CIA and joined him. High up in an office tower, Sarah and Casey put on a fight to convince Volkoff, and in the midst, they agree that Sarah can throw Casey out a window so he can land on a platform. (Season 4, Episode 12: "Chuck Versus the Gobbler")

Casey whispers, "I'll be fine, promise."

Sarah responds, "Okay, but you better be fine, or else I'll really kill you."

• By the end of season four, as noted earlier, when Sarah's life is at risk, Casey tells Chuck: "You're Chuck Bartowski, the second-best spy I ever worked with. Now, you're going to go save the best." (Season 4, Episode 24: "Chuck Versus the Cliffhanger")

Chuck Business Tips

Can a partnership really develop from complete distrust to one of complete trust, as is the case with how things went with Casey and Sarah?

It's rare, but it can happen with the right individuals and the right circumstances.

But I have my doubts that a true partnership – that is, one in which trust and respect exist, each person contributes from their strengths, and each accepts the other's plusses and minuses – can develop by bringing a consultant into a workplace, for example, to run managers and employees through staged trust-building exercises. While there's always room for advice and assistance in building business partnerships, the real work is done, well, in the real-world trenches.

Casey and Sarah had to prove that they had each other's back, were focused on the mission, could get the job done together, and ultimately, cared about the other person.

But as already noted, setting up a business as a partnership often is advised against. The challenge with many partnerships is not so much the Sarah and Casey issue of building trust and a partnership from a beginning of distrust. Instead, it's maintaining the partnership and trust as time passes, even when the partnership begins with some level of trust.

Partnerships usually are born from recognition that each individual somehow compliments the other. In another business venture, I had a successful run in a partnership because, while I was the writer and researcher, my partner excelled in sales. That business partnership eventually ended, but we remain friends today.

Again, though, one is left wondering if that is the exception. Writing in the *Financial Times* on July 12, 2011 ("When two's company but three's a crowd"), Luke Johnson offered a positive take on the business partnership. He wrote: "Such relationships help spread the load and usually make the journey a more enjoyable one." True. However, later in the column, he acknowledged that "it is estimated that more than half of all business partnerships fail."

As a result, every bit of advice I have ever read about setting up partnerships has focused on a partnership agreement laying out how decisions are made, and how the partnership eventually would be dissolved.

From my own experience, the best partnerships come when the partners have experience working together, and therefore understand how each person functions. That way, fewer surprises or disagreements should pop up to put the enterprise in peril. If you can manage some kind of test run, that's a plus for entering into a partnership in the business world.

"I don't trust anybody."

- General Beckman

13
Trust Versus Work? Co-Workers, Employees and Bosses

Given that *Chuck* is focused on the life of spies, the issue of trust comes into play. After a chapter on building a partnership, let's address trust in business even more directly.

It's important to understand the role trust plays in our economy. As a virtue in the marketplace, trust means having confidence in the honesty, reliability, and integrity of market players. It speaks volumes about our free enterprise system that a stranger can walk into a small business, for example, that he has never patronized before, and yet generally trust that he will be served well, dealt with fairly, and leave with a product that does what it is supposed to do.

Underlying this broad example of trust in a market economy is trust within a business. Owners and managers have to be able to trust that their employees will be honest and reliable, while working hard and, particularly these days, working smart.

The same goes for employees being able to trust that the boss is going to make wise and ethical decisions that will sustain and grow the business, while also treating each individual with respect.

And finally, much the same goes for co-workers. Employees have to be able to rely on each other to get the job done and to do the right thing.

The following *Chuck* examples touch on various aspects of trust in the workplace.

• In the very first episode, Sarah tells Chuck, "I need you to do one more thing for me... Trust me, Chuck." (Season 1, Episode 1: "Chuck: The Pilot")

By the second episode, since Casey and Sarah do not trust each other, each urges Chuck not to trust the other. (Season 1: Episode 2: "Chuck Versus the Helicopter")

The challenges of trust continued with the arrival of one of Sarah's former partners, Carina (Mini Anden). Again, Chuck is pulled in two different directions. Sarah tells him not to trust Carina, while Carina says she can be trusted. (Season 1, Episode 4: "Chuck Versus the Wookie")

It should be obvious that a business and its workers will not reach their true potentials if staff members are concerned about being undermined by each other. It's tough enough keeping an eye on the opposition without having to guard against the guy at the next desk stabbing you in the back.

• The role of trust in a partnership is nicely summed up by, of all characters, Jeff. (Season 2, Episode 14: "Chuck Versus the Best Friend")

When Devon and Ellie are looking for a wedding band, Jeffster auditions. When it comes time to finally play, Lester is afraid. Jeff tells him: "Partnership is trust."

Lester says, "I can't do this, man."

Jeff assures, "You can. I know you can." And just a bit later: "Ever had a dream that's never come true? I am asking you to sing, not for yourself, do it for me."

In their own dysfunctional and creepy ways, Lester and Jeff have come to trust each other to the point that one friend is willing to place his dream in the hands of the other. That's a powerful statement on trust.

• Due to the importance of the fight against Fulcrum, General Beckman admits that she does not want the Intersect out of Chuck's brain, contrary to what she previously promised. Beckman notes how many agents have been lost and how powerful Fulcrum is, and points out that only Chuck's team has "found a hole in their armor." She declares, "I need you. It's time to become a spy." (Season 2, Episode 17: "Chuck Versus the Predator")

Disappointed, Chuck later tells Sarah that the spy life is not his future. He declares, "I will get my life back."

Sarah asks, "We're still a good team, right? You still trust us?"

Chuck says, "I trust you. Of course, I do."

Sarah tries to reassure, "I'm on your side, Chuck."

And Chuck replies, "I know."

At the same time, though, Chuck's response is half-hearted, and he is hiding information from her.

Meanwhile, the General asks Casey about Sarah. She says, "I want everything you have on her and Bartowski, video surveillance and your unedited report."

Casey asks, "Don't you trust me?"

Beckman responds, "I don't trust anybody."

Team Bartowski is in a bad place here. A degree of distrust is germinating between Chuck and Sarah. Meanwhile, General Beckman has failed miserably as a manager in this instance, as she goes back on her word with Chuck (even if it is perhaps for the right reasons), thereby planting those seeds of distrust between Chuck and Sarah. For good measure, she explicitly tells Casey, one of her employees, that she trusts no one, including him.

• Emmett convinces Morgan that if a review of the Buy More goes well, then corporate will "promote me out of this hellhole," which is what they both want. So, Morgan gets the Buy More workers to behave. (Season 2, Episode 20: "Chuck Versus the First Kill")

Morgan asks, "How do I know that I can trust you?"

Emmett responds, "You don't. But I want out and you want me out. So, let's make a deal."

But Emmett actually was setting up Big Mike. Emmett becomes the store manager. Morgan concludes, "I trusted the wrong person."

To be clear, this is not trust. Instead, it is an example of deep distrust leading to a kind of "deal with the devil" – including manipulation of other employees – in order to accomplish what both sides want. It should not surprise anyone, including Morgan, that such a trustless deal fails in the end.

• When Chuck invites Sarah's old spy team – the CAT Squad – to their engagement party, it turns out that the team no longer trusts each other due to an old incident. One person is suspected of being a traitor, but the assumptions underlying those suspicions turn out to be wrong. (Season 4, Episode 15: "Chuck Versus the Cat Squad")

The distrust between the four CAT Squad members is a classic example of rumor and duplicity undermining a team. Accusations, denials and subterfuge nearly destroy their ability to work together.

• Chuck and Sarah are frustrated at not having any new mission assignments. At the same time, they are not happy about Casey keeping secrets, and working with a new team. Chuck and Sarah worry about no longer being the A team and becoming the B team, behind Casey's. (Season 4, Episode 18: "Chuck Versus the A-Team")

As a result of the lack of clarity and the distrust generated by that cloudiness, an unproductive kind of competition develops between the teams that undermines the overall organization.

• The wedding planner that Chuck and Sarah hire winds up conning them out of their money. In order to catch the thief, they mislead Beckman to gain access to government resources. But the lie quickly spins out of control, and Chuck and Sarah forfeit the trust of the General and the U.S. government when the lie is revealed. Beckman orders them: "You are not to pursue anyone or anything until you have earned back the trust of the United States government." (Season 4, Episode 21: "Chuck Versus the Wedding Planner")

In the end, the question here is simple and straightforward: Can your co-workers or employees be trusted not to use company resources for their personal pursuits?

Chuck Business Tips

"Trust no one" might work for science fiction television shows, Sixties' hippies, or conspiracy theorists, but it cannot work in the business world.

Business needs solid teamwork. And teamwork comes from trust. Managers must create a productive working environment in which trust can take root and flourish.

At its core, that means managers must make establishing trust a priority through example. Employees must see, through action, that the manager considers trust a critical component the firm's culture and success.

That community of trust then needs to be further reinforced by acknowledging and rewarding actions that grow out of or build trust among the workforce; and by making clear through feedback mechanisms and performance measures that actions undermining trust will not be tolerated.

The issue of trust in the workplace too often goes ignored by managers. That is most often the case in places where a cutthroat, do-anything-to-get-ahead business philosophy prevails. But when trust is proven to be important, it generates additional benefits.

Olivier Serrat, writing in the August 2009 *Knowledge Solutions* ("Building Trust in the Workplace"), published by the Asian Development Bank, summed up the benefits of a high degree of trust in the workplace:

> Since trust among interacting parties is the foundation of effective relationships, it stands to reason that organizations can reap benefits from strengthening it. As a matter of fact, high-trust environments correlate positively with high degrees of personnel involvement, commitment, and organizational success. Decided advantages include increased value; accelerated growth; market and societal trust; reputation and recognizable brands; effortless communication; enhanced innovation; positive, transparent relationships with personnel and other stakeholders; improved collaboration and partnering; fully aligned systems and structures; heightened loyalty; powerful contributions of discretionary energy; strong innovation, engagement, confidence, and loyalty; better execution; increased adaptability; and robust retention and replenishment of knowledge workers. Nothing is as relevant as the ubiquitous impact of high trust.

Don't be fooled by General Beckman missing the boat and Jeff seemingly getting it on trust. If teamwork and loyalty, not to mention profits, are deemed to be important for an enterprise, then trust can in no way be ignored.

"We wake up in some of the best dumpsters in this city."

- Jeff

14

The Business Versus Jeffster: Sex, Drugs, Gambling, Booze and Violence in the Workplace

All of the potentially explosive actions that a business owner or manager wants to keep out of the workplace, Jeff and Lester can be counted on to bring into the Buy More.

Consider the following, disturbing number of examples, which, by the way, is in no way an exhaustive list of inappropriate undertakings by Jeffster.

• Jeff and Lester are secretly recording peeks at the chests of women who come into the Buy More. (Season 1, Episode 13: "Chuck Versus the Marlin")

Later, Jeff, Lester and other workers are gambling on thumb wars.

• Jeff and Lester volunteer to take over the job of interviewing for a new "Green Shirt," that is, a Buy More sales person. But they turn it into a "casting couch" situation by claiming that the position is a high-paying modeling opportunity to become the "Buy More babe." They proceed to do a series of inappropriate interviews with beautiful women. (Season 2, Episode 15: "Chuck Versus the Beefcake")

• In a stressed out state, Chuck "flashes" with the Intersect and mistakenly hits Lester with a roundhouse kick.

Lester says that being hit was "the thrill of being alive... The electrified sensation of pain coursing through my face was like an adrenaline shot to my soul. It made me feel like a man, maybe for the first time since my Bar Mitzvah." As a result, employees start hitting each other, and eventually running a fight club in the back of the Buy More. (Season 3, Episode 4: "Chuck Versus Operation Awesome")

Morgan says, "We cannot have this, guys. Come on, there are insurance issues."

• Lester and Jeff are upset that they were left out of a plan to use Jeff's "stalker van." (Season 3, Episode 12: "Chuck Versus the American Hero")

Jeff declares, "Do they have any idea how much stalking experience I have?"

Lester responds, "If only they did, Jeffrey. You're very prolific. You're the Picasso of creepiness."

Later, when Jeff and Lester take matters into their own hands, Jeffrey records his "stalker's log."

• On a mission, Casey is drugged, but still escapes from his former team who are trying to kill him. He mistakenly calls Jeff and tells him that he needs extraction and is hiding in a dumpster. (Season 4, Episode 5: "Chuck Versus the Couch Lock")

Jeff says, "Don't worry, Casey, I know that dumpster." Jeff then calls Lester with a Nerd Herd emergency.

Later, Jeff tells Casey: "We wake up in some of the best dumpsters in this city."

• When Morgan needs video about Sarah for Chuck and Sarah's engagement video, Lester volunteers, "We have over 1,250 hours of Sarah-related footage." (Season 4, Episode 23: "Chuck Versus The Last Details")

• Big Mike gathers his Buy More workers together to go over the ground rules of the store holiday party. There are only two, and both apparently have resulted due to bad experiences with Jeff during past parties. (Season 1, Episode 13: "Chuck Versus the Crown Vic")

Big Mike declares, "Rule number one, Jeff, no spiking the eggnog."

Jeff asks, "Can I bring my own?"

Big Mike says, "No. Rule number 2, Jeff, no holding the mistletoe over the women and copping a feel."

Chuck Business Tips

Jeff and Lester would rank as the perfect storm for a manager. They partake in all of the actions in the workplace that offend customers, disgust co-workers, undermine productivity and loyalty, perhaps break the law, and generate lawsuits.

Indeed, Jeff and Lester seem to be all about sexual harassment, drug use, the abuse of alcohol, gambling, and violence. That being the case, they are the extreme examples of why business owners and managers must have clear policies established and communicated about what kind of behavior is not tolerated in the workplace. This goes back to the previously noted code of ethics for a business, and having each employee read and sign such a code.

From the manager's perspective, it must be made clear that gambling, sexual harassment, drug use, alcohol, and violence are not allowed in the workplace, and that consequences exist for such undertakings.

But while Jeff and Lester provide many laughs, how serious is the use of drugs and alcohol in the workplace?

On its "Workplace Substance Abuse" webpage, the Occupational Safety & Health Administration sums matters up this way: "Of the 17.2 million illicit drug users aged 18 or older in 2005, 12.9 million (74.8 percent) were employed either full or part time. Furthermore, research indicates that between 10 and 20 percent of the nation's workers who die on the job test positive for alcohol or other drugs." For good measure, OSHA points out that small businesses are at greatest risk: "They are less likely than large companies to have programs in place to combat the problem, yet they are more likely to be the 'employer-of-choice' for illicit drug users. Individuals who can't adhere to a drug-free workplace policy seek employment at firms that don't have one, and the cost of just one accident caused by an impaired employee can devastate a small business."

Many firms obviously decide that more is needed beyond, for example, an anti-substance-abuse declaration in a code of ethics. Tapping into legal and human resource expertise to design and execute substance abuse testing can make sense. But again, it is small firms that will be unable to afford such programs. In the end, as with so many decisions in owning and managing a business, the costs and benefits must be weighed.

From a career point of view, though, this should be a no-brainer. The various behaviors indulged in by Jeff and Lester can only undercut career advancement. Unfortunately, though, whatever might be the reasons, and despite the risks and potential problems to personal and professional well-being, people still make bad decisions. And managers must be on guard, as those poor choices often affect others, including employers.

"But haven't you personally given me the order to kill that commie crackpot on three separate occasions?"

- Casey

15
Casey Versus the Business Plan: Changing the Mission

For many entrepreneurs, the business plan is a critical tool for success.

If an owner is seeking equity investment or a loan, a clear, compelling and substantive business plan ranks as a must.

But even if an entrepreneur is not seeking outside funding, or has simply not reached that stage of growth as yet, the business plan can still be a valuable vehicle for clarifying thinking on a business idea; outlining goals and how to achieve them; and assessing how a business is developing.

A business plan must answer many questions. But two are essential. The first comes at the very start: Is the basic business idea sound? A second question comes later: Is a business plan etched in stone, or should it be adjusted or even changed significantly depending on the circumstances?

Chuck offers a couple of examples that relate to these questions.

• The CIA had a plan to take down Alexi Volkoff and his entire criminal enterprise by inserting Sarah as a double agent. But Chuck is done watching from the sidelines and risking his family. He decides a new plan is needed. (Season 4, Episode 13: "Chuck Versus the Push Mix")

Chuck tells Morgan, "We're going to take down Volkoff."

Morgan declares, "I'm in... Which guns do we grab?"

Chuck, opening a closet, responds, "No guns, we need..."

Morgan finishes, "...office supplies?"

Chuck says, "No, Morgan. We need a plan."

They proceed to create an elaborate and complex wallboard of action.

Chuck observes, "This is going to work."

Morgan unconvincingly replies, "Yeah, it is. Of course, it is. It's a good plan." But he adds later, "Do you think this is what they call a suicide mission?"

Chuck tries to reassure, "Morgan, this is going to work. I promise."

After Chuck leaves the room, Morgan says, "Oh man, we're going to need some help."

• The leader of the small nation of Costa Gravas collapses while in the United States. Premier Alejandro Goya took over the nation in a 1974 communist coup. The exchange between General Beckman and John Casey is illustrative. (Season 3, Episode 3: "Chuck Versus the Angel de la Muerte")

Beckman: "The Costa Gravan premier is listed in critical condition."

Casey: "Outstanding. Crack the bubbly?"

Beckman: "No. I want you to go to the hospital and guard against further threats to his life, natural or otherwise."

Casey: "But haven't you personally given me the order to kill that commie crackpot on three separate occasions?"

Beckman: "And three times you have failed to complete your orders... Our relations with Costa Gravas have changed, Colonel. The premier is here to announce plans to open his nation up to democratic elections."

Casey: "Oh, and you believe that..."

Beckman: "Our duty is to stop anyone who would stop him from going through with his plan. Understood?"

Casey: "Yes, ma'am."

While Casey is still known as Angel de la Muerte – the Angel of Death – in Costa Gravas, he now risks his life to protect the premier.

Chuck Business Tips

In terms of creating a business plan, while the format certainly can vary, the basics include:

• Executive summary. Preferably a one-pager that highlights the key points in the plan.

• Business and industry description. This section explains the business in detail, including the product or service, potential customers, industry details and trends, competitors, and how the enterprise will gain from existing or creating new opportunities.

• Management team. Who are the people behind the business? This matters as much as the idea itself, as investors recognize that they ultimately are investing in people.

• Market plan. This section lays out the strategies for gaining customers, sales, pricing and distribution.

• Operations. This describes how the firm functions on a day-to-day basis, including staff, location, facilities, production procedures, and quality controls.

• Financial factors. The firm's short-term and long-run expectations on profitability must be explained, and supported by income and cash-flow statements, and a balance sheet.

Going through this process aids the entrepreneur tremendously in terms of thinking through all aspects of the enterprise. This can clarify things not just for the business owner, but also for the management team, as well as potential investors or lenders.

In contrast, Chuck's wallboard plan is so complex and filled with unanswered questions that Morgan is left with little faith in its success. Unfortunately, messy, question-generating business plans are not all that unusual in the business world.

Meanwhile, General Beckman and Casey have seen the market change dramatically, with a former enemy now a friend. As a result, the plan they have been operating under for decades makes no sense, with the new plan pointing in the opposite direction.

The General seems to accept the change in matter-of-fact fashion. She has her new orders, and despite those orders being contrary to what she did for decades, orders are orders and she will do her duty.

Casey has a more difficult time. He was invested emotionally and philosophically in the mission to take down a "commie crackpot." And he clearly is not pleased with the new direction. However, though still griping along the way, Casey does his job, to the point of risking his own life for a person he had been ordered to eliminate before.

In the marketplace, change is the reality in which businesses must operate. And sometimes that change can be radical.

Consider the example of the now-defunct Borders Group Inc. I explained the key points in an August 2011 column in *Long Island Business News*:

How did this firm go from the high-flying ranks of an industry innovator to filing for bankruptcy protection this past February to selling off all of its assets? It's not all that unusual in a dynamic, competitive marketplace. A combination of bad business decisions, a failure to keep up with industry changes, and a poor economy closed the book on Borders.

Keep in mind that Borders was a key player in changing the industry by spreading book superstores across the nation, particularly in the 1990s. Shoppers appreciated the huge selection, along with the inviting store environments. Indeed, it was not that long ago that Borders was being blamed for the demise of the small, independent bookstore.

But poor decision-making took hold in the 2000s. Most glaring was Borders' inability to grasp the significance of two earth-shaking changes to the industry.

First was the impact of Internet book sales. As it struggled online, Borders handed over the operations of its Internet business to top-competitor Amazon in 2001. By the time Borders retook its online reins in 2008, Amazon.com was the Internet book king. It's hard to imagine a worse decision in the book business.

But Borders managed to match this level of incompetence by coming to e-books far too late. By the time Borders partnered with Canada's Kobo Inc. to introduce the Kobo e-reader last year, it was nearly three years after Amazon.com had launched the Kindle. Borders also was beaten to the market by Barnes & Noble's Nook and Apple's iPad.

Broadband Internet and e-books rank as the biggest revolutions to hit the book universe since Gutenberg's printing press in the 15th century – and Borders missed the boat on each.

But still more contributed to the fall of Borders.

The firm's debt load exploded to drive overseas store expansion and stock buybacks. *The Wall Street Journal* reported that the firm's debt grew from $159 million in 2001 to $554 million in 2008, while "Barnes & Noble eliminated all its $667 million in debt" over the same time.

For good measure, the company jumped from CEO to CEO. Four CEOs in three years meant ever-changing business plans, and a company in trouble with no idea of where it was going.

Put these choices together with the one of the worst recessions since the Great Depression running from December 2007 to mid-2009, followed by one of the poorest recoveries, and it's not surprising that Borders entered bankruptcy early this year.

Borders was unprepared for dramatic technological and economic changes. Throw in other bad decisions, and the business went under. If that can happen to an industry leader, think about how dramatic market and economic changes can impact a small business.

Therefore, a business plan should not be etched in stone.

Instead, returning to your business plan once a year can help in assessing how the market has changed, how the business has performed, whether you have gotten off track, and what changes, if any, might be needed.

"You know, I don't know one person who responds positively to being yelled at."

- Chuck

16
The Buy More Versus Employee Pay: How *Not* to Compensate or Motivate Your People

Business owners and managers need to motivate employees. The incentives at work for people at all levels of the organization must be understood, and then these need to be aligned, or re-aligned, with the primary purpose of the business, that is, to maximize profits.

Therefore, owners must design incentives so that managers' interests line up with the owner's interests. In turn, managers must understand incentives so as to maximize and direct efforts from their employees.

Consider examples of trying to motivate employees and co-workers in the *Chuck* series.

• Big Mike decides that it's time to motivate the Green Shirts in the Buy More. (Season 1, Episode 5: "Chuck Versus the Sizzling Shrimp")

He gathers his workers together, and declares, "Sales are down people. There's too much horsing around. Now, what this team needs is some good old-fashioned competition... Twenty-four hour sales competition starting now. First prize: iPhone. Second prize: Large pizza, two toppings... Third prize is you get to keep your job. Last prize: You're fired."

Morgan proves that he is a terrible salesman, running in last place, until Ellie comes to his rescue by buying gifts for the family and saying that Morgan helped her.

Morgan tells Big Mike: "I sold over $700 of stereo equipment. Puts me in second place. Means somebody owes me a pizza with two toppings."

Big Mike says, "The pizza's for me, partner."

Morgan asks, "Do I get an iPhone?"

Mike answers, "I don't even get a free iPhone. Do you think I'd give you jerks one?"

Morgan responds, "There are no prizes?"

Big Mike declares, "And no one's getting fired. The competition was to get you bums to work harder. Looks like it worked."

• Emmett decides to reinstate the Buy More "Employee of the Month" contest, based on customer comment cards, with a wall photo and a "bonus prize." (Season 2, Episode 9: "Chuck Versus the Sensei")

After walking by a sign on the wall outside the break room declaring, "Through these halls walk the smartest employees in the world," Morgan tells Jeff and Lester, "Alright, just to be absolutely clear, our position on 'Employee of the Month' is that we don't care. Are you guys with me?"

Jeff says, "Yep, not caring, not a rat's ass."

Lester adds, "Not a fat and/or hairy one."

But Jeff then wonders, "Wait, why don't we care, again?"

Morgan replies, "Because 'Employee of the Month' is a scam. And working hard is for suckers. Think about it. So, you work hard. Sales go up. Sales go up, shareholders get rich. Shareholders get rich and we get what exactly?"

Lester responds, "He said something about a prize."

Morgan continues, "Your face on a wall... No, thank you. No, you know what, keep your stupid stooge prize."

Jeff asks, "So, we get nothing?"

Morgan says, "Emmett's going to get all the credit. He may even get a promotion."

Morgan offers an alternative. "We have our own contest. A side bet. We see who can get the lowest score on their comment cards."

Later, in response, Emmett tells Jeff, Lester and Morgan: "Since none of you seem to be taking this 'Employee of the Month' contest very seriously, I must abandon the carrot and use my stick... From now on the employee with the lowest scores will close up every Saturday night for an entire month."

In the end, the "Employee of the Month" prize turned out to be a 65-inch flat screen television. The Buy More workers who listened to Morgan, and did not compete, were not pleased.

• After giving Casey the particularly difficult assignment of bringing in Sarah and Chuck dead or alive, General Beckman offers Casey his pick of assignments and promotes him from major to colonel. (Season 3, Episode 21: "Chuck Versus the Colonel")

• When the Intersect is not working for Chuck, the CIA brings in Agent Jim Rye (Rob Riggle) from psych-ops to get the Intersect working in him once more. (Season 4, Episode 8: "Chuck Versus the Fear of Death")

Rye uses brutal physical and anxiety creating psychological tactics in his attempts to get the Intersect working, including a sneak Ninja attack, pain therapy, and finally, the "pure fear of death."

Unfortunately, Rye, using the real threat of immediate death to get the Intersect working, winds up getting shot and dying himself.

• On a mission, as Casey is chasing a criminal, he yells at Chuck to remotely close a set of doors before the bad guy gets away. (Season 2, Episode 9: "Chuck Versus the Sensei")

In the midst of Casey's pursuit, Chuck says, "You know, I don't know one person who responds positively to being yelled at."

But the bad guy winds up escaping.

Chuck Business Tips

In each of these examples, the efforts to motivate or incentivize people go awry.

While less than ideal, including in terms of how he communicates the policy, Big Mike's sales competition has some basic merits. For this particular group of workers, a sales contest with an iPhone as top prize and even a second place award of a two-topping pizza, is not a bad idea. For good measure, it's necessary to make clear that there are negative consequences to poor performance. Of course, Big Mike undermines the entire effort and wipes out his own credibility as the contest turned out to be phony.

As for Emmett's "Employee of the Month" contest, it's undermined not only by the unwillingness of Morgan, Jeff and Lester to work hard for any reason, but also because of Emmett's complete lack of credibility as a manager. As a result, any positive plan Emmett puts forth is viewed with deep suspicion by the workers.

The General Beckman case is important to note. She understands what motivates her employee, John Casey. It is not monetary compensation that spurs him. What is Casey all about? At one point, Sarah asks Casey about his priorities, and he responds, "God, country, duty, Corp." (Season 4, Episode 3: "Chuck Versus the Cubic Z")

Beckman understands who he is, and offers Casey a promotion and choice of assignments.

In contrast, the last two examples show that the CIA and Casey do not know how Chuck ticks, and therefore, do not know how to motivate him to get the job done. Chuck is not a person who responds to shouting or any kind of negative impulses.

How can managers align incentives and motivate workers? On the monetary front, options include bonuses, raises, commissions, promotions, and pay tied to profitability or share prices. There's also the negative side of the compensation coin, if you will, including the lack of any raise or bonus, pay cuts, or termination.

But again, it is critical for managers to understand what ultimately drives each employee. Money can be just part of the equation, along with security, flexibility in terms of work time, promotions, and the ability to make important decisions – or perhaps, even a two-topping pizza.

"You men are both excellent stalkers."

- Morgan

17

The Buy More Versus Wasting Talent: The Hannah Example

Some managers fail in identifying talent for the organization.

Sports, of course, serve up excellent examples of jobs completely reliant upon identifying talent. From team management to coaching staffs to scouts, a central aspect of work is to identify, develop and tap into the best talent.

In some workplaces, however, managers can either neglect or even ignore entirely the responsibility of identifying and developing top talent. For many, it might be a matter of insecurity, i.e., not wanting to groom a person who might take their own job.

For others, it's just an inability to think beyond the immediate, day-to-day activities, with no vision for improving and building the business.

At the Buy More, there was a glaring example of wasted talent:

• Over a series of four episodes, Chuck and the Buy More are introduced to Hannah (Kristin Kreuk).

Chuck meets her on a mission while flying in first class to Paris, and they hit it off. (Season 3, Episode 5: "Chuck Versus First Class")

It turns out that Hannah was just fired from a high-paying job that involved computers and international travel. As they part ways, Chuck says, "Hannah, if you ever find yourself in Burbank – and I don't know what the chances of you finding yourself in Burbank are – but if you do find yourself in Burbank, and you're still without a job, my assistant manager owes me about a million and a half favors. Although I have to warn you, you will be terribly over-qualified for the job."

She takes Chuck up on his offer.

As Chuck starts to give Hannah a tour of the Buy More, she says, "I know this isn't my dream job, but I thought that while I'm here I'd be the best Nerd Herder you have." (Season 3, Episode 6: "Chuck Versus the Nacho Sampler")

Meanwhile, since Morgan likes her, he tells Jeff and Lester: "You men are both excellent stalkers. I need you to use your skill set to find out everything there is to know about Hannah, okay – likes, dislikes, everything."

Lester says, "Consider her stalked."

However, it's clear that Hannah is attracted to Chuck. She asks him to teach her how to be a Nerd Herder, but his spy work pulls him away. Hannah even follows him to a museum, thinking that it's a Nerd Herd job, but it turns out to be a CIA mission. As a result, Chuck winds up having to leave Hannah to fend for herself, effectively throwing her under the bus, much to her anger and frustration. (Season 3, Episode 7: "Chuck Versus the Mask")

Finally, when Hannah believes that Chuck is going to be with her, Chuck realizes that he still loves Sarah. And when Chuck breaks up with Hannah, acknowledging that he has been dishonest, she tells him, "I have dated a lot of liars before, so I usually know how to spot them. But you,

you are like the best I have ever seen." (Season 3, Episode 8: "Chuck Versus the Fake Name")

Chuck Business Tips

The case of Hannah is an over-the-top example of wasting talent, not to mention treating a nice person poorly.

Hannah indeed is grossly over-qualified for the Buy More, yet she takes her work responsibilities seriously, and wants to be the best Nerd Herder she can. But Chuck not only fails to guide and train her for Nerd Herd work, due to his CIA missions, he winds up abandoning her.

In addition, Morgan, as assistant manager, is far more interested in dating Hannah, rather than managing and helping her in the workplace, to the point that he even taps into the stalking talents of Jeff and Lester to get more information about her.

Eventually, Chuck's personal life – specifically, his love for Sarah and subsequent break up with Hannah – chases Hannah away from the Buy More altogether.

In contrast, the best managers are unafraid to identify and develop talent. They become mentors to individuals who they see as having potential.

In an essay on leadership ("What Makes a Leader?" *The Essentials: An Introduction to the Most Enduring Ideas on Management from Harvard Business Review*, Harvard Business Review Press, Boston, 2011), Daniel Goleman explains:

> It has repeatedly been shown that coaching and mentoring pay off not just in better performance but also in increased job satisfaction and decreased turnover. But what makes coaching and mentoring work best is the nature of the relationship. Outstanding coaches and mentors

get inside the heads of the people they are helping. They sense how to give effective feedback. They know when to push for better performance and when to hold back. In the way they motivate their protégés, they demonstrate empathy in action.

The manager as mentor and developer of talent helps the business grow, while actually boosting her own career due to an enhanced reputation for both herself and the firm. As her position flourishes, so do the individuals she helps mentor. They advance and reach their potential. It's a win-win for everyone.

"Well, you didn't wet yourself this time. It's an improvement."

- Casey

18
The NSA Versus Employee Training: Casey on Training Workers

Is an NSA assassin the best choice for training new workers? Probably not.

Consider the following:

• The first lesson that Casey teaches Chuck is simple and straightforward for a new worker. After Chuck defuses a terrorist's bomb, Casey advises, "Don't puke on the C4." (Season 1, Episode 1: "Chuck: The Pilot")

• After Emmett saves Big Mike from choking on a doughnut, the Buy More institutes an emergency preparedness class. Morgan, Jeff and Lester try to steal the CPR test from Captain Awesome, as well as cheating off Chuck during the written test. (Season 2, Episode 6: "Chuck Versus the Ex")

• Casey is given the assignment of making Morgan weapons and field ready. And Casey decides that Morgan can be taught everything he needs to know in the Buy More. (Season 3, Episode 15: "Chuck Versus the Role Models")

Casey tells Morgan: "There are three qualities that make for an effective field agent." Subversion, stealth and strength.

Morgan's first lesson in subversion is to get the phone number of a beautiful woman in the store. Casey notes, "A spy must be able to manipulate any target at any time. In the field, it can make the difference between life and death." Morgan fails.

In the second lesson, Morgan must use stealth to remove Big Mike's key card while he is sleeping at this desk. Again, Morgan fails.

Finally, during gun training in the CIA Castle base secretly located below the Buy More, Morgan compares it to playing a video game. But when he fires, the gun jumps out of his hand.

• Casey puts Morgan through a mock interrogation to show him how to withstand torture. Casey's assessment: "Well, you didn't wet yourself this time. It's an improvement." (Season 4, Episode 18: "Chuck Versus the A-Team")

After Casey leaves, though, Morgan admits, "Oh, no, I peed a little bit."

Chuck Business Tips

Again, it is critical to keep in mind that your employees *are* your business. Worker training, therefore, should in no way be neglected, or treated as a mere afterthought.

Nor, as we see from Casey and Emmett, should it be done in a haphazard or seat-of-the-pants manner, or in a way that is open to circumventing important lessons.

A systematic method for training employees must be established. While different types of businesses have varying degrees of training needs, their processes must still be comprehensive, rooted firmly in the real world of the business and the jobs at hand, and designed to communicate and teach the firm's mission, goals, ethics and culture.

An owner of a manufacturing business that I did a project with years ago thought it necessary to offer his factory workers citizenship, English and basic math classes, which he believed would aid those individuals and his business.

Plenty of businesses also see value in aiding their employees in earning college or graduate degrees. For example, some businesses have even decided that it makes sense to partner with and/or provide space to colleges and universities that in turn offer employees training and classes, often leading to degrees.

On Long Island, for example, Dowling College (where I teach in the MBA program as an adjunct professor) has the Dowling Institute, which partakes in these kinds of partnerships. As explained on the Institute's webpage:

> The Dowling Institute has teamed with leading corporations around the globe to develop and implement educational and training programs that are conducted at the work site or at Dowling's … campuses. Each program is customized to meet the company's specific needs and fit the employees' work schedule. Subject matter may involve technical, managerial and computer skills, or customer service training. The Dowling Institute also works with companies to provide credit

programs, in which employees can conveniently earn their Bachelor's or Master's degree in business, either on-site or at Dowling's campuses.

It also should be recognized that the learning process never really ends, and again depending on the work, ongoing training will be needed to refresh, expand and update employee skills and thinking. The key is to focus on quality at the start, and to reinforce and build quality in subsequent training efforts.

Not puking or peeing oneself might be enough for early stages of spy training, but a heck of a lot more will be needed in the business world. The best training program is designed to train the individual for success, which in turn should feed into the success of the business.

"Harry Tang is drunk with power."

- Morgan

19
Business Versus the Number Two Guy: Harry, Morgan, Lester and Emmett

Not only is Chuck Bartowski over-qualified for his Nerd Herd work at the Buy More, but he also has had to suffer through working for a string of assistant managers who clearly are far less competent than he is.

While not the case in small businesses, who by their very nature have to be lean and mean, the nature of larger firms, i.e., more workers doing more and different tasks, means there will be layers of management. And the lower layers of management are critical for business success, as these are the managers who tend to be in direct contact on a day-to-day basis with the vast majority of the workforce, not to mention customers.

Consider the following examples of four individuals who have served as Buy More assistant managers.

• Assistant Manager Harry Tang sets out new rules and regulations for the Buy More. Morgan says Harry "is like the dark lord Sauron from *The Lord of the Rings*, only except the ring of power, he's taken over control of the assistant managership." As Morgan and Chuck are complaining to each other about the new rules, Harry makes clear his managerial tone when saying, "I'm sorry fellas, but is this the Talk More?" (Season 1, Episode 7: "Chuck Versus the Alma Mater")

Harry also imposes a staggered lunch schedule. In the break room, Morgan and Chuck become distressed that they can no longer have lunch together. Morgan declares, "Harry Tang is drunk with power."

Listening, Anna suggests, "He could have an accident. I'm just saying, I know a guy very reasonable. His rates, I mean."

When Harry arrives, he warns, "I'm going to be the one who breaks you, Grimes. You know why? Because you're soft, like pudding."

• In a brief period as assistant manager, Lester Patel tells the staff: "Because we did our time together in the trenches, I know what screw ups most of you are. For example, Jeffrey, you spend the hours of three and five sleeping in stall two of the employee bathroom... Morgan, no more borrowing company DVDs and then just re-shrink wrapping them." He adds, "Please, call me Mr. Patel, or boss, or for our Latin friend, El Heffe." (Season 2, Episode 2: "Chuck Versus the Seduction")

Later, the workers are gathered in the break room, and Lester says, "If you're not going to respect me, you will fear me. May I present the Wheel of Misfortune."

Morgan spins and lands on "You're FIRED." But Anna quits, and the rest of the workforce follows and walks out. They return, but only with their demands met.

• Emmett Milbarge is sent by Buy More corporate. He interviews and evaluates each worker, asking, "Why do you belong at the Buy More?" (Season 2, Episode 5: "Chuck Versus Tom Sawyer")

It turns out that Emmett is made assistant manager, and tells the employees, "I'm afraid this branch is sick. And not the kind of sick that can be fixed with a Band Aid. What this Buy More needs requires a surgeon. Someone who doesn't mind getting up to their elbows in guts. And that's exactly what I'm going to do. I'm going to reach in, wrap my fingers around the disease, and rip it out."

• As assistant manager, Morgan confronts a belligerent group of workers led by Lester, and offers his management philosophy. He says, "Here are the first, second and third rules of the Buy More. Do what you're told. Do it with respect. Or ... I'll fire you." (Season 3, Episode 4: "Chuck Versus Operation Awesome")

After challenging Morgan and getting fired, Lester begs for his job and seems to have learned his lesson. Morgan decides, "Okay, you're rehired, but you're on probation – double secret."

Chuck Business Tips

As an employee, few things rate as more frustrating than dealing with a manager who not only has an inflated opinion of himself and is carried away with power, but also is clearly less qualified than the employee.

In the cases above with Harry, Lester and Emmett, each has no clue as to how to deal with employees, and has failed to earn the respect of anyone working at the Buy More. They try to make up for failing to earn respect largely by trying to instill fear. Fear, however, is an inadequate management philosophy.

It's interesting to note that Morgan, after being a Buy More slacker himself for a long time, has grown into the role of assistant manager. Put a slightly different way, his three management principles come down to: do your job, respect others, and if you cannot manage these basics, lose your job. While the details and execution obviously matter, that's not a bad starting point for becoming a good manager.

But in the end, it's all about the example that managers set. In a brief September 8, 2011, column ("Becoming an Effective Manager") at Suite101.com, Tara Wagner, who works for a company that provides professional services to small businesses, summed matters up perfectly:

> One of the best ways to be an effective manager is not to tell people what to do, but to show them. If you expect everyone else to follow the rules and don't do so yourself, you will only cultivate an image of yourself as a lazy slave-driver, making it impossible to gain the respect and trust of your employees. It's up to you to set a good example, and when you're productive and motivated, they usually will be too.

Why do Harry, Lester and Emmett fail to earn the respect of Buy More workers? There's your answer.

"I often think about meats and cheeses."

- Lou

20

Lou Versus Lester: The Passion of the Entrepreneur

Entrepreneurship and the investment that fuels such crucial risk taking are what drive the economy forward.

No matter how big a business gets – including such current-day leaders as Wal-Mart, Microsoft and Apple – each was at one time a small, entrepreneurial venture. For good measure, most businesses in the U.S. are smaller firms. The Small Business Administration's Office of Advocacy has reported, for example, that of the 27.5 million businesses in the U.S. in 2009, 99.9 percent had fewer than 500 workers.

In *Chuck's* first four seasons, only one true entrepreneur was introduced, while another regular character had entrepreneurial dreams, but lacked the common sense needed by entrepreneurs.

• A woman named Lou enters the Buy More with a cellphone that is not working. Lou is freaking out because, as she puts it, "my entire life is in this thing." (Season 1, Episode 8: "Chuck Versus the Truth")

Chuck tries to calm her, saying she can trust him to fix it. When Lou again starts to get upset, he advises, "No, no, don't go there. Come back. Go to a happy place. Is there something that you think about that quiets the voices that are in your head?"

Lou says, "Turkey, muenster cheese, egg bread, grilled."

Chuck asks, "Was that a sandwich?"

Lou responds, "Yeah, they're my passion."

"It sounds pretty delicious," says Chuck.

Lou declares, "I own a deli in the mall. I often think about meats and cheeses."

• When the Jeffster band is playing outside the Buy More, Big Mike observes, "That's quite a wad of cash you hustled on Buy More property."

Lester responds, "Whoa, this is our dream. We're on break. You can't touch us."

Big Mike says, "I don't want to touch you. I want to help you. In case you forgot, I know a thing or two about management. You're too good to be playing outside a chain electronic store. If I was your manager, you might be playing inside a chain electronic store."

Lester responds, "Yeah, we've already played the Buy More. We don't need you."

But Jeff says, "I'm listening... having a manager means having respect."

Lester warns, "How many times do I have to tell you? Art: good. Commercialism: bad, evil, weird, chubby."

Lester then walks away from Jeffster.

Later, Big Mike tries to assure Lester: "I'm a man, a man who once had a dream, too. You ever heard of Earth, Wind & Fire?"

Lester nods, "Yeah, they jammed."

Big Mike tells him: "For a short time in 1988, we were called Earth, Wind, Fire & Rain. I was Rain."

Impressed, Lester finally says, "Where do I sign?"

Chuck Business Tips

When I'm in the midst of marketing and selling a book, my oldest son often jokes by shaking his head and declaring, "You're going commercial."

My response? "Darn right, I'm trying to go commercial."

The point of any entrepreneurial venture is to go commercial, if by "commercial" one means trying to appeal to and generate a large volume of sales from the largest number of consumers. After all, the point is success.

"Going commercial" also does not necessarily mean diminishing the artistic quality of one's product or service. After all, consumers ultimately want the best product for the best price.

Lester doesn't grasp this notion. He wants success, but is unwilling to take the steps needed to achieve it. Of course, the fundamental problem is that Jeffster isn't any good as a band.

Lou, however, is the type of entrepreneur who understands what it takes to go commercial. She is passionate about her deli, and obviously works to offer customers the best sandwiches around.

Indeed, Lou is willing to go above and beyond to get the best ingredients, as illustrated when she illegally imports salami, in order to get around government customs regulations that make no sense, to get the tastiest meats. Even as he goes off to save Chuck and Sarah, Casey takes a second to tell Lou: "By the way, miss. Your pastrami's delicious." (Season 1, Episode 8: "Chuck Versus the Imported Hard Salami")

Lou is a passionate and smart entrepreneur.

"Thank you for saving me. I appreciated the tank."

- Sarah

21
The CIA Versus Love:
Love in the Workplace

Love at work? It's anything but unusual these days.

Indeed, many people meet and fall in love in the workplace, and wind up getting married. Just look at Chuck and Sarah.

In real life, it's apparently not all that unusual at the CIA. In March 2011, NPR's WBUR.org reported on the authors of *The Company We Keep: A Husband-and-Wife True-Life Spy Story*: Robert and Dayna Baer. It was noted:

> Unlike many couples, the Baers met while they were part of a covert team of CIA operatives sent into Bosnia to protect a high-ranking CIA official, who had been targeted for assassination by Hezbollah... It's no secret, they say, that CIA employees often date each other. "You have someone you can talk to about what you do," Dayna says. "You can share things with them. It's much easier to have a relationship with someone inside the CIA versus the outside."

But there can be challenges for managers when love, or at least sex, blossoms among employees.

• While at work, Chuck and Morgan are talking about Chuck's love life. But Morgan stops listening, in order to become entangled in a kiss with his girlfriend, Anna. Later, Anna and Morgan get distracted from work due to having a relationship disagreement. (Season 1, Episode 10: "Chuck Versus the Nemesis")

Meanwhile, the spy workplace is disrupted by Sarah's former partner and love interest, Bryce Larkin, returning seemingly from the dead. And this comes after Sarah had kissed Chuck, thinking they were both about to die. Chuck is thrown off, as is Sarah.

Both of these instances show how romance can be disruptive to work. Morgan and Anna partake in inappropriate behavior, and competing love interests send the team off kilter when it comes to Sarah, Chuck and Bryce.

• At another point, in typical direct fashion, General Beckman asks Chuck: "I'd like to know if your relationship with Agent Walker is compromising your job performance?" (Season 2, Episode 18: "Chuck Versus the Broken Heart")

Chuck wonders, "How do you mean? What does that mean?"

The General answers, "Has your situation gotten too complicated?"

Chuck nervously says, "What? With Sarah? No. God, no. No. Sarah Walker is a pleasure to work with. A delight even."

Beckman continues, "I want facts. I don't care about your feelings."

Chuck says, "What feelings?"

"These feelings," replies the General, and then she shows him video on a series of encounters in which Chuck tells Sarah that he has feelings for her.

Beckman explains, "My job is to make sure you're protected without interloping emotional complications from my team. We're going to have to do a 49-B."

Bewildered, Chuck asks, "Okay, if you could just tell me what a 49-B is, that would help..."

But the General cuts off communications. Later, Chuck finds out that a 49-B occurs when an agent, in this case Alex Forrest (Tricia Helfer), is sent to evaluate another agent's – Sarah's – performance.

Agent Forrest eventually reports, "Based on my observations, Agent Walker is far too emotionally entwined with the asset. Her decisions weren't made with respect to established protocol. She always places the subject's feelings above orders."

Beckman tells Sarah: "Agent Walker, thank you for your dedication to this mission... But as of right now, your services are officially terminated. Report back to Langley at 0900."

Sarah is told to have no contact with Chuck, but when trying to leave him information about his father, she discovers that Chuck is in trouble. And it turns out that since Sarah understands and cares about Chuck, she is the one who can and does save him.

Chuck attempts to explain to Beckman: "I'm sorry, but isn't the important part of being my handler making sure I stay alive? ... Um, General, what I'm trying to say is that I think that maybe because my relationship with Sarah is so... You know, we're close. We care about each other. That's what I'm trying to say. And I know it's not protocol or whatever, but it's those feelings that wound up saving my life."

Beckman responds, "Agent Forrest diagnosed your emotional connection as a liability. But I suppose it can also be an asset to the, well, asset. You may resume your post, Agent Walker."

General Beckman is in a position where she has to determine if love – or the possibility of love – in the workplace is a plus or a minus for the mission. To her credit, she makes her final decision based on all of the available information, not just one report from an underling.

• When Sarah tells Chuck that she wants to run away with him, including away from his new spy life, Chuck says yes. But when they meet weeks later at a train station, Chuck tells Sarah that he wants to stay and become a spy. He says, "Sarah, there's an entire facility here dedicated and designed to turning me into Intersect 2.0. I mean think about that, me, a real spy. You know, living a life of adventure and doing things that really matter." (Season 3, Episode 1: "Chuck Versus the Pink Slip")

In the following episode, Sarah, obviously feeling hurt, tells Chuck: "You need to learn to ignore your emotions. Spies do not have feelings. Feelings get you killed. You need to learn to bury them in a place deep inside." (Season 3, Episode 2: "Chuck Versus the Three Words.")

One of the risks of workplace relationships is that when those relationships run into problems, work can suffer. And on the flip side, decisions made at work can affect the relationship.

• Chuck is concerned that Shaw is going to murder Sarah. As a result, Chuck pulls out all the stops to save her, including heavily armed troops, air and armor. (Season 3, Episode 13: "Chuck Versus the Other Guy")

For now, Shaw fools all, except Chuck, into thinking he's not out to kill Sarah. Chuck appears to have gone way overboard in his response. But Sarah says, "Thank you for saving me. I appreciated the tank."

Later, Sarah finally admits that she loves Chuck. While drunk, Chuck asks, "Just once for the record, Sarah, do you love me?"

Sarah says, "Yes... Chuck, I fell for you a long, long time ago. After you fixed my phone, and before you started diffusing bombs with computer viruses. So, yes."

Not long after that, Chuck and Sarah decide to quit the spy game for each other. Each thinks this is what the other wants. But even as they run, neither one can resist secretly trying to stop the bad guys they happen to come across. Eventually, Chuck and Sarah realize that they want each other and the spy life. (Season 3, Episode 14: "Chuck Versus the Honeymooners")

Beckman tells Chuck and Sarah: "I must caution you that allowing your private life to interfere with your professional one can be dangerous. But off the record: It's about damn time."

The next step for Chuck and Sarah is to observe a CIA married couple – Craig and Laura Turner (Fred Willard and Swoosie Kurtz) – to learn how to be a CIA couple. The Turners, however, offer little in terms of positive lessons, as they turn out to be traitors. (Season 3, Episode 15: "Chuck Versus the Role Models")

Chuck Business Tips

In the case above, General Beckman captures the basics of the situation, i.e., that risks exist when personal and professional lives mix, but in the end, decisions must be made both by the individuals involved and by the organization.

Business owners and managers need to be realistic about romance in the workplace. It's going to happen whether they like it or not. The question is: How is the business best protected from any negatives that might develop as a result?

Policies can be designed to govern not just sexual harassment, but also situations where attraction is consensual and mutual, including making clear what types of behavior are off base while at work. One might be tempted to think that such matters are basic common sense, but common sense in so many human endeavors, especially when emotions run high and deep, can be lacking.

The business also can be at the mercy of the ups and downs of the personal relationship. That is, arguments and break ups can spill over into the workplace. This is where managers must fall back on establishing a professional culture in the business. In addition, a policy, whereby once co-workers are involved personally, they are, if possible, separated in terms of their day-to-day work involvement with each other, is a consideration.

Any company policies or guidelines established regarding workplace romances must be fair, clear and applied uniformly across the enterprise, and obviously should not run awry of the law.

Finally, while individuals like to think that their personal relationship is no one else's business and only affects each other, that, of course, is not the reality. On the job, it's easy to envision jealousy and disputes arising over real or perceived preferential treatment due to a personal relationship developing between two employees.

Managers must be tuned in to such possibilities, and nip any problems in the bud. But this is another case whereby the culture of the business should be established in such a way that this kind of behavior is frowned upon throughout the business.

"... nerdy, emotional, into his family and friends..."

- Chuck

22
Chuck Versus the Interview: The Angst of Interviews

Few people I know love the interview process for a job, and that includes the interviewer and the interviewee.

The manager can be stressed about getting the right person for the job. After all, make the wrong decision, and the consequences can range anywhere from mild headaches for managers and co-workers to a debacle for the firm, not to mention reflecting poorly on the person who made the wrong hiring decision.

Getting it right, of course, means that the firm benefits, and the manager receives kudos for making the right choice.

Meanwhile, the job seeker might be feeling all kinds of pressures, from being currently unemployed to seeking a new job in order to get out of a bad situation. There's also the anticipation that comes with being interviewed for an outstanding opportunity.

Chuck offers three interesting interview situations.

• After Chuck turns down the Buy More assistant manager job, Big Mike gives him the task of interviewing people for the position as a punishment. (Season 2, Episode 1: "Chuck Versus the First Date")

While Chuck is interviewing Anna, she asks Morgan, her boyfriend, to leave and then tries to play footsy with Chuck to make Morgan jealous.

Jeff's resume is written in red marker on napkins, and apparently reveals disturbing facts.

For some reason, Lester winds up slipping into his Godfather impression during the interview.

Chuck winds up delegating the selection of assistant manager to Morgan, who sets up a steel cage match between Jeff and Lester in the back of the Buy More.

• Chuck thinks he's done with the CIA. So, he heads out on interviews, but his experiences turn out to be very strange. (Season 4, Episode 1: "Chuck Versus the Anniversary")

One interviewer falls asleep. Another throws up. The third goes into convulsions. And the fourth leaves for coffee, but never comes back. The final interviewer gets a call during the interview, and then has security escort Chuck from the room.

Unbeknownst to Chuck, General Beckman undermined each of his interviews because she wants him back working with the CIA and NSA.

• General Beckman orders Chuck "to find more Chucks" for the Intersect project. (Season 4, Episode 19: "Chuck Versus the Muuurder")

Four candidates are sent to Chuck to be evaluated. One candidate, Brody, is described by Chuck as "nerdy, emotional, into his family and friends" – just like Chuck. Casey says, "Dear God, there's another one."

For the interviews and evaluation process, Casey is put in charge of physical testing, Sarah psychological evaluations, and Morgan in charge of cultural knowledge.

They are seeking another Chuck, since Chuck is the only individual who has succeeded with the Intersect.

Chuck Business Tips

Once again, the Buy More shows what *not* to do. Big Mike shirks his managerial responsibilities by pushing the interview process off on Chuck. As it plays out, the interview process winds up having nothing to do with discovering which person would be right for the job.

As for the latter two cases, Chuck is in a favorable position in that he has an employer seeking him out specifically (though to the point of undermining his other interviews), and later, that he is recognized as so valuable that he is tasked with finding more employees just like himself.

It's important to establish a systematic interviewing process designed to weed out the undesirable candidates and advance the best aspirants. That can be done internally, for example, with the human resource department communicating the position to be filled, sorting through resumes, doing initial interviews, and then passing the best candidates on to the manager or department with the job need for final interviews. Or, it can involve an outside employment service, or headhunter, doing most of the initial legwork.

In the late stages of the interview process, it can be worth having the candidates interview with various leading team members for evaluations as to how the person might fit in or not fit in, such as with Casey doing physical testing, Sarah's psychological evaluations, and Morgan assessing cultural knowledge in the search for the next Chuck.

In terms of the actual interview, the manager needs to be thoroughly prepared, from reviewing resumes to having a solid handle on what's needed for the job, and be ready to ask relevant questions. Afterwards, references should be checked, and the Internet can serve as a valuable additional source of information.

Finally, when the decision is made, move quickly to offer the job to the best candidate. While time and resources are needed to make the right selection for a job, it never ceases to amaze me how many organizations delay the process for an unnecessarily long period of time. That can mean missing the opportunity to add a valuable employee.

"You're fired. Pack up your hard drives and get out of here."

- Morgan

23
The Buy More Versus the CIA: Terminating Employees

Opposite the hiring decision, of course, is the firing decision.

It's never easy to fire someone, but at times, it is an unfortunate necessity, whether because the business is suffering due to poor decisions, a bad economy, or both; the individual engaged in unethical or unlawful activity; or the employee simply is not getting the job done, even after receiving the proper feedback and being given a fair chance to succeed.

Consider instances of firing people in *Chuck.*

• A new Intersect is being readied. As a result, Chuck is no longer needed. As noted in an earlier chapter, Beckman orders Casey to eliminate Chuck, saying, "We can't have another Intersect wandering around Los Angeles getting into trouble." (Season 2, Episode 1: "Chuck Versus the First Date")

• At a later occasion, Chuck is coming up woefully short in terms of his training to become a spy. (Season 3, Episode 1: "Chuck Versus the Pink Slip")

After a life-or-death simulation is over, in which Chuck fails to get the job done, Beckman declares, "This isn't working out."

Chuck responds, "Look, General, I realize that we've had our setbacks. I do. But let's not dwell in the past here. I'm convinced I can be a great spy. I know it."

Beckman counters, "We've spent millions of dollars to get you up and running as our new Intersect agent. It's not working... It's over. Our Los Angeles field unit will keep an eye on you until a final decision can be made regarding your status."

Chuck says, "Wait. Hold on just a second here. Are you saying you're firing me, General? Do you have any idea what I gave up for this?"

"Good-bye, Chuck," says Beckman.

As he protests further, Beckman has Chuck tranquilized.

• In terms of running the Buy More, the workers do not respect Lester as their assistant manager. Big Mike tells Lester: "The problem is, they don't fear you... Don't you watch Animal Planet? Find the wounded gazelle and pounce. Thus endeth the lesson." (Season 2, Episode 2: "Chuck Versus the Seduction")

While highlighting this scene earlier, it certainly applies again here.

When the workers are gathered in the break room, Lester says, "If you're not going to respect me, you will fear me. May I present the Wheel of Misfortune."

As noted previously, Morgan spins and lands on "You're FIRED." But Anna quits, and the rest of the workforce follows and walks out. They return, but only according to their own terms.

• Another example pointed to earlier must be noted here when talking about firing people.

When Morgan is assistant manager, he also is unable to control the Buy More staff. Big Mike tells him: "First rule of Big Mike management: You can't be afraid to pull the trigger." (Season 3, Episode 4: "Chuck Versus Operation Awesome")

Morgan tells Lester, "Your behavior will no longer be tolerated. So, here are the first, second and third rules of the Buy More. Do what you're told. Do it with respect. Or … I'll fire you."

Lester tells him: "You don't have the cojones."

Morgan declares, "You're fired. Pack up your hard drives and get out of here. The rest of you, back to work."

After Lester begs and seems to have learned his lesson, Morgan decides, "Okay, you're rehired, but you're on probation – double secret."

Chuck Business Tips

A reluctance to fire someone, no matter what, can lead to big problems. I've seen situations in which an unwillingness to fire an individual who clearly must go has weighed down entire organizations.

Managers need to understand that by failing to pull the trigger on a necessary firing, while perhaps being nice to the particular individual in the near term, can put the work of others in the company and the entire enterprise at risk.

General Beckman obviously is not afraid to make the tough decision to fire an individual. And she does so without remorse – even in fictitious *Chuck* spy fashion, willing to have an employee terminated in the fullest sense of the word when called for.

Lester, however, makes the firing decision without any semblance of a link to job performance or the overall well being of the firm. That does nothing to aid the business. Indeed, to the contrary, it only undermines morale and performance.

As for Morgan, he gets it right in this case. He explains clearly what's expected, and when Lester not only fails to meet those requirements, but mocks them, Morgan fires Lester. The firing of Lester, and perhaps the terms of his re-hiring, work to make the Buy More a better store. Morgan has clarified what is expected and what will not be tolerated from employees.

In addition, we probably all know people who never saw it coming when fired; they were shocked. It's noted time and again in management literature and in the business world that if an employee is surprised when fired, then the manager has not done his job. Employees should be provided with performance reviews and feedback. That includes when their work is somehow coming up short. That's not only being respectful to the individual, but is positive for the firm. After all, a business benefits if it can correct misbehavior or poor performance, rather than having to go through the costly and unfortunate process of firing someone, and hiring and training a replacement.

Finally, if termination is necessary, the process should be done with respect. That means doing it face to face, and not doing it over the telephone, as was the case, apparently, when Yahoo Inc. fired Chief Executive Carol Bartz in September 2011, as noted, for example, in a September 9, 2011, *Wall Street Journal* article ("Bad Call: How Not to Fire a Worker" by Dana Mattioli, Joann S. Lublin, and Rachel Emma Silverman). It's also important to explain to the individual why they are being terminated. The authors noted in the *Journal* article:

One study of nearly 1,000 terminated workers in Ohio found that workers were 10 times more likely to report suing their former employer if they were given no explanation of why they were dismissed than workers given a complete explanation.

Firing can be a necessity, but there's no reason why the process cannot be done with basic dignity. It should not be handed over to a stealthy NSA assassin.

"Other men wear collared shirts all day, while I get to wear a great big BM on my chest."

- Big Mike

24
Sales Versus the Buy More: Advertising and Sales Strategies

The crew at the Buy More overwhelmingly is clueless about how to operate a business, and that certainly includes crafting sales and advertising strategies.

While again amusing and outrageous, nuggets of truth exist in these Buy More examples as to what *not* to do when trying to boost sales.

• As Morgan struggles during a sales competition, Jeff and Lester suggest "the wounded raccoon." (Season 1, Episode 5: "Chuck Versus the Sizzling Shrimp")

While Morgan is helping and being nice to a customer, Lester taunts, "Look at the little man, so weak, so pathetic."

Jeff chimes in, "And you wonder why you're last in sales and about to get fired."

Lester piles on, "Maybe if you spent your time selling merchandise instead of trolling for phone numbers, maybe you wouldn't be flat broke and living with your mother, and be forced to pick leftovers out of the garbage so that you could eat."

The customer asks for her phone number back from Morgan and leaves. Morgan asks, "Are you kidding me, what was that?"

Jeff says, "The wounded raccoon."

Lester explains, "You berate and humiliate the salesman in front of the customer, like so, which I thought we did very well. And the customer feels so bad that they'll buy anything. It's the 'pity sale.'"

Jeff adds, "Always wondered if it worked. Guess not."

Lester says, "No, it does not. It does not. Wow."

• With Big Mike away on a fishing trip, Lester comes up with a new plan to "revolutionize" Buy More sales. He explains, "From now on, we're gonna work with our customers to create mutually agreed upon prices." In practice, however, that turns out to be whatever the customer wants to pay. (Season 2, Episode 4: "Chuck Versus the Cougars")

The results? Lester declares, "We moved the largest volume of big ticket merchandise in four years. But no matter how many times I crunch the numbers, we're still out 2,700 bucks."

Chuck says, "Well, you forgot to carry the one, so, actually, it's 3,700."

The Buy More crew decides to host a kegger party, and charge by the head, to make up the shortfall.

• The Buy More is in trouble. Big Mike tells Lester, "My main man Moses, founder of the Buy More himself, called. Said if we don't see a spike in numbers, and fast, they're gonna close the store." (Season 3, Episode 19: "Chuck Versus the Ring, Part 2")

Lester makes a suggestion: "May I propose something that I rarely do in life myself? Tell the truth... If in fact we are going out of business, why not just tell that to our most loyal customers?"

"You mean have a going out of business sale. Slash the prices, sell everything to juice the books? That's crazy."

Lester: "Crazy... good?"

"There may be a brain under that mop after all," Big Mike agrees.

• Morgan says, "Wow, is it really big BM day?"

Big Mike, dressed in a green and yellow BM costume, replies, "That's the best kind of day there is."

Big Mike is frustrated that the competitor, Large Mart, has been copying the Buy More's promotions, so he is going to hand out flyers in a big BM suit (supposed to represent the Buy More) to sell televisions.

But Morgan says, "You do not have to sell yourself like this."

Big Mike replies, "Say what? Other men wear collared shirts all day, while I get to wear a great big BM on my chest. That's job satisfaction."

Large Mart employees wind up kidnapping Big Mike in his big BM in retaliation for Buy More workers kidnapping Kevin Bacon, the Large Mart's cute pig. Lester says, "Weirdly, an adorable little pig attracts more customers than a large man wearing a yellow and green BM. Call me crazy."

Chuck Business Tips

Of course, poorly thought out sales plans are destined to fail, including bizarre efforts along the lines of the wounded raccoon, allowing customers to set prices without regard to costs, and an ill-conceived advertising strategy that emphasizes a big BM.

Sales strategies need to be rooted in identifying and understanding the customer, fully knowing your product or service, having a strong knowledge of the market and industry, taking note of what competitors do right and wrong, mastering fundamental sales skills, and using all tools available to advance sales.

Interestingly, one sales strategy tried at the Buy More at least has some relationship to common sense.

It's not unusual to have food samples for customers to try in retail establishments involved in the food business, from the corner deli to large retailers. Big Mike decides to go that route to recover from a purchasing error.

Instructing the Buy More staff, Big Mike says, "Due to a clerical oversight, we received triple the number of Crock-Pots I may have intended... El Segundo School of Finance has taught me when you're trying to sell a house, bake some cookies. Make the place smell familiar. Gonna do the same thing here, except with gumbo. Folks smell something cooking in that Crock-Pot makes them wanna buy the fool thing." (Season 3, Episode 8: "Chuck Versus the Fake Name")

Proving that even a stopped clock is right twice a day, Big Mike stumbles on the basics of a sound sales strategy. Unfortunately, in the real world of business, few enterprises can afford to simply stumble upon the right sales idea.

*"How many Marines you know would go up against a
Bengal tiger unarmed?... You'd have to be a complete
idiot."*

- Casey

25
Morgan Versus Courage: The Big Moments

Is "courage" an overworked word? For example, how often is it used when referencing the act of an athlete on the playing field or a decision made by a coach?

True courage means facing pain or even life-threatening danger without being sure as to how things are going to turn out. The first thing that comes to my mind when thinking about courage is the American military fighting for our nation and the freedoms we enjoy.

But on a lesser level and in a very different context, there are decisions made by individuals in the business world that can be called courageous. For example, the acts of starting up a business or investing in a new business rank as courageous, as they are undertakings packed with risk.

There are other instances calling for courage in business. Consider examples from *Chuck*.

• Workers from another store – Mighty Jocks sporting goods – invade the Buy More in order to play the Madden

'09 NFL video game on a big screen and at no cost. (Season 2, Episode 3: "Chuck Versus the Break Up")

Lester, as assistant manager, and other Buy More workers are afraid to tell them to leave. Morgan is sent in, but one huge jock, Mitt (played by former NFL lineman Michael Strahan), threatens to "smush" Morgan's face.

Morgan later suggests to Lester: "What about a plan that does not require direct confrontation?" When they cut off the electric in order to end the jocks' video game, Mitt gets very upset that his game-winning drive was ended and declares, "After work, I'm gonna kick both your asses."

But after Mitt insults Anna, Morgan pours a soda over his head. And when they wind up in the back of the Buy More in the cage, and it looks like Mitt is going to crush Morgan, Anna steps in with martial arts, and takes Mitt down.

• As noted before, Morgan has always dreamed of being a Benihana chef in Hawaii. He finally stands up to the abuse doled out by store manager Emmett, and quits the Buy More to pursue his dream job and asks Anna to go with him. At one point, Lester declares, "God, I admire him." Morgan leaves the Buy More to applause. (Season 2, Episode 21: "Chuck Versus the Colonel")

• After Morgan fails all of the CIA training to become weapons and field ready, he and Casey are returning to their respective apartments when they come across bodies and a loose Bengal tiger. (Season 3, Episode 15: "Chuck Versus the Role Models")

Morgan tells Casey: "This country needs men like you Casey. Okay? What do I do? I sell refrigerators. You know, I mean, if I die, they'll shop at Large Mart. Big deal. But there is a way that I can serve my country... I'm luring the tiger into Ellie and Awesome's apartment... Now listen to me, no matter what you hear in there, promise me you will not go in after me." And he springs forward before Casey can do anything. The tiger chases him into the apartment, up the stairs, and Morgan jumps out the second floor window to Casey and safety.

Casey tells Morgan that he passed his field tests despite failing each category. Casey says, "You got balls... How many Marines you know would go up against a Bengal tiger unarmed?... You'd have to be a complete idiot."

• With the Buy More wired with explosives and the store full of customers, Morgan is captured and handcuffed to a chair. Casey tells Morgan that he has to break his own thumbs to get loose in order to pull the firm alarm and get people out of the store. He does so. But just as Morgan reaches it, the alarm is set off. (Season 3, Episode 19: "Chuck Versus the Ring, Part 2")

• Casey and Morgan head to Iran to save Chuck and Sarah. When Casey gets captured, it's all up to Morgan. After making sure that his friends lift their feet out of water on the ground, Morgan grabs a live electrical cable hanging down from the ceiling and pushes it into the water. The bad guys are taken down, but so is Morgan. He actually dies for three seconds. (Season 4, Episode 5: "Chuck Versus the Couch Lock")

Chuck tells Morgan, "Buddy, that was the single bravest thing I've ever seen anyone do."

Chuck Business Tips

As illustrated by Morgan, sometimes courage comes from places one might least expect.

Morgan not only exhibits that highest form of courage, when an individual is willing to sacrifice himself to save others, but he also provides examples of courage in business.

First, in his confrontation with the Mighty Jocks goons, Morgan provides a reminder of the risk that business owners and employees might face with unruly customers, or members of the public bent on doing harm. For example, businesses must have protections against potential criminal acts. Confronting unruly customers or potential criminals requires courage.

Second, Morgan shows the courage of taking a risk to pursue one's dream when he chooses to quit the Buy More in order to try to become a Benihana chef in Hawaii. Changing careers requires courage.

Third, when confronted by the Bengal tiger, Morgan not only exhibits courage by placing his life in peril, but he also alludes to a very different kind of business courage in admitting that another individual (Casey) might be more valuable to a company compared to what he (Morgan) brings to the table.

A good manager comes to recognize the importance of high character among employees. Over the first four seasons of *Chuck*, the growth in Morgan's character is apparent, taking him from just another slacker to a person that steps up in tough times by exhibiting courage. That's the kind of person you want in your business.

"Remember, family and friends are everything. Money, greed, and power are a dance with Satan, and he looks like me."

- Volkoff

26
Personal Life Versus Work Life: Keeping Work in Perspective

Finding the balance between personal life and professional life can be very difficult.

When I was covering a conference for my newspaper column several years ago, I struck up a conversation with a Wall Street executive seated next to me. The discussion started with what we each did for a living, and somehow ended up on families.

What stuck with me was his clear annoyance at an upcoming family vacation. His unmistakable preference was to stay at work, rather than go with his wife and kids to a theme park. As we parted ways, I probably stepped over the line by saying something along the lines of: "Hey, go on vacation with your kids, work will always be there."

Of course, in a competitive, 24/7 economy, it's often easier to dish out such advice than actually taking it and living it. For many, there is the reality that one's career is the primary, or only, means for supporting one's family.

My acquaintance, and the rest of us, might learn something from Chuck Bartowski – a man with a job he has come to love, but with family and friends he cares about even more.

• Ellie finds out that Chuck is a spy, sees their father gunned down by Agent Shaw, and helps save Chuck from the Ring. After that, she asks Chuck: "What are we gonna do?" (Season 3, Episode 19: "Chuck Versus the Ring, Part 2")

Chuck says, "We're gonna go after them and we're gonna get them. We're gonna take them down, the Ring and Shaw, for what they did to dad. They are not gonna get away with this."

Ellie replies, "Okay, and then you're done."

"What?"

She continues, "As a spy. This life, this job. Chuck, I made a promise to protect you and I can't do it. Not from this. So, you finish it, and then you're done."

Chuck struggles, "Ellie, I can't..."

"We are all that we have left, Chuck, and I'm not gonna lose you, too."

"Okay. I'll get Shaw and I quit. I promise."

• When Chuck is kidnapped and on the edge of death, Sarah is willing to do anything to save him. She ignores orders and international law, tortures a prisoner, imprisons Casey, battles her way across Thailand, and fights in a brutal arena. Finally, Casey and Morgan join her, and they raid the camp where Chuck is being kept and experimented on, finally saving Chuck. (Season 4, Episode 9: "Chuck Versus Phase Three")

It's Sarah's love for Chuck that saves him, and his love for her is where Sarah finds that she is more than a spy.

• In turn, after Sarah is poisoned, Chuck risks everything to get the antidote. He breaks Volkoff out of prison, and takes on the CIA – with the help of his family and friends. (Season 4, Episode 24: "Chuck Versus the Cliffhanger")

When Chuck parachutes in with the antidote to save Sarah, Decker, a shady, unethical CIA dude, and his men try to stop Chuck. But Volkoff's Russian military troops also parachute in to back up Chuck.

Decker accuses Chuck: "Russian special forces, you really are a traitor."

Chuck replies, "Just for the day."

Decker warns, "You're done."

Chuck says, "I quit. Now get out of my way." He sprints into the hospital for Sarah.

Chuck gives up the CIA spy life for Sarah.

Of course, after Volkoff gives Chuck and Sarah his entire company for a wedding present – which, as Chuck puts it, is worth "a cool billion" – the newly married Bartowskis buy the Buy More, and invite Morgan and Casey to join their new private security firm to fight bad guys.

The next step for Chuck is becoming an entrepreneur, and it's a family business.

Chuck Business Tips

If it came down to your business or career versus your family, which would you pick?

The answer to this question will reveal what you value most in life, if addressed honestly.

The answer for Chuck is clear: Family and friends come first, no matter how much he loves being a spy. Indeed, he is willing to risk everything for the people that matter most in his life. And it turns out to be the same for Sarah, along with Morgan, Casey, Ellie and Devon.

In real life, hard decisions sometimes have to be made between business and family. It's not unusual, for example, to read or hear about great entrepreneurs who were not so great when it came to their families. Divorces and neglected children, unfortunately, are part of these tales.

But for most, this is a false choice. Many business owners and managers have discovered that they don't have to choose between family and business. Instead, through prioritization, balance, planning and communication, they find time for both career and family. Of course, that process is not always smooth and simple, but it is doable.

These kinds of decisions will be dictated by values. After Alexi Volkoff starts looking to make up for his past evil deeds, he tells Chuck and Mary Bartowski (Chuck's mom played by Linda Hamilton): "Remember, family and friends are everything. Money, greed, and power are a dance with Satan, and he looks like me." (Season 4, Episode 20: "Chuck Versus the Family Volkoff")

If business and career are driven solely by greed and the pursuit of power, that says something about one's values and what decisions will be made. The threat of dancing with the devil is quite real.

But if money and career success are viewed as tools for achieving greater things, such as supporting one's family and providing security, and are recognized as the results of providing goods and/or services needed or desired by others, then very different decisions likely will be made.

At the close of the fourth season, from the ruins of their previous careers, Chuck and Sarah are married, and embark on a new career of running a business together, with their close friends Morgan and Casey onboard – family, friends and business.

If Chuck and Sarah can do it, why not the rest of us? Of course, a "cool billion" in seed money would be a big help. But without big bucks, millions of individuals work and succeed at owning and/or running a business, having a successful and rewarding career, while at the same time valuing family. Indeed, the family often is involved in running the business.

At the time of this writing, it's going to be fun and interesting to see what the fifth and final season of *Chuck* brings in terms of business lessons at the good old Buy More and a new private spy firm, both owned by Chuck and Sarah.

27

A Salute to "Chuck" for Family and Business

Chuck ranks as a unique television show.

Like other quality series, it excels at smart storytelling, establishing characters that people care about, and being darn funny. But what sets *Chuck* apart from many television shows in recent times is its appreciation for what one might call old-time values, namely, family, patriotism, and friendship.

Throughout its television run, *Chuck* has struck a consistent tone of sacrifice and love of country. Amidst all of the laughs is an unmistakable willingness among the main characters to put all on the line for each other and to protect the American people.

In addition, the importance of family is central to the show. Chuck protects his sister and brother-in-law, and has risked all to find his father and mother. His friend Morgan has grown to be a brother. Morgan was there for Chuck throughout the good and bad times of life, especially when Chuck's mother and father left, and when Chuck got kicked out of Stanford.

Finally, by being alongside Chuck, the lone-wolf, super-spy Sarah comes to understand what she has missed by not having a family, and has come to appreciate family through her love for Chuck.

While parts of the show's humor are not always friendly for the pre-teen set, in most other ways, Chuck ranks as a family-friendly, family-reinforcing television show. Like I said, that's pretty rare these days.

At the same time, unfortunately, *Chuck* has been ratings challenged throughout its television run. Whether that's due to its difficult Monday night time slot against some other big hits or for other reasons, it has meant the show seems to have been perpetually on the cancellation bubble.

And here is where Chuck provides another business lesson.

Zachary Levi and fans of the show have engaged in rather unique campaigns to keep the show coming back.

In 2009, there was the Subway campaign to get *Chuck* renewed for a third season. As described in an April 23, 2009, TVGuide.com article by reporter Joyce Eng:

> As the geek-tastic comedy remains in limbo for a third-season pickup, fans hope they have all the fixings of an inspired movement to save the series. The Finale and Footlong campaign implores fans to go to Subway before Monday's season (series?) finale, buy a $5 footlong sandwich and leave a note in the suggestion box. Why Subway? The restaurant chain is one of *Chuck's* main sponsors and was notably featured in a recent episode.

Later in April 2009, TVGuide.com reporter Erin Fox added:

> A massive fan campaign is underway to earn NBC's *Chuck* a Season 3 pick-up — and it has even found series star Zachary Levi himself

stepping behind the counter of a Subway sandwich shop in London to assemble footlongs for scores of fans... Levi remarks while standing before a fervent crowd, "You see, NBC? This is what happens when you might cancel a show that people care about!'"

Chuck fans were at it again in 2011, looking to secure a fifth season. On the *Entertainment Weekly* website – EW.com – in April 2011, reporter Sandra Gonzalez noted:

This week marked the beginning of a Twitter campaign spearheaded by fan site We Give a Chuck that aimed to let the show's advertisers know, well, that they exist...

On Monday — and for the next few weeks, apparently — the group sent Tweets to the advertisers during the show in hopes of getting their attention. (Example: "@Tide just saw your ad on @NBC's #Chuck. Thx! You support Chuck, I'll support you PS-I use the to-go stick all the time! #NotANielsenFamily") And oddly enough, they worked. Diet Pepsi's Twitter account responded to the outpour that evening, saying "Wow! #chuck fans are awesome! Thanks for all the support!!!! #notanielsenfamily."

In their bubble show analysis, EW's Lynette Rice and James Hibberd said the show (which averages 5.9 million viewers) had one major strength: "[It's] perhaps NBC's only drama that can blow up Twitter." And it looks like the fandom is going to do exactly that to accomplish their mission, which they tend to take as seriously as Chuck takes his.

For good measure, Chuck has been a television haven for product placements, including Subway (big time), Tide, and Honda.

Some people might find such campaigns and placements annoying or intrusive. In contrast, I find them interesting and innovative, as well as amusing at times.

First, product placements bring realism to stories. In my own novel, *Warrior Monk: A Pastor Stephen Grant Novel*, I inserted real products and actual places to enhance the story and provide additional avenues for readers to relate to the characters and story. (And I did so without compensation, by the way.)

Interestingly, on August 16, 2011, a *Wall Street Journal* report noted that viewers generally prefer product placements over television ads. Testing reactions to digital placement, according to Mark Popkiewicz, CEO of MirriAd, "proved surprising. 'They don't want commercials, they don't want pre-rolls, they don't want overlays. Given the choice, the majority prefer placement to commercial breaks. From a broadcasters point of view that is a huge plus. It gives them far more inventory to sell without a penalty to the consumer or the audience.'"

Second, it follows that product placements provide additional revenue that fund television shows and movies. That means more choices for viewers.

Third, fan campaigns, such as the *Chuck* Subway and Twitter efforts, communicate important information to television networks and producers. When creating, funding, producing, and renewing television series, it should not only be about ratings, but also about who is watching, where and when they are watching, and the intensity of interest. Getting feedback beyond Neilson ratings has to make for better decision-making.

So, ironically, while the Buy More serves up lots of examples of bad business decision-making, *Chuck* itself has offered some positives on how a television business venture is able to continue by more completely engaging advertisers and viewers.

While playing "what if," it's reasonable to argue that without the Subway and Twitter campaigns, *Chuck* might never have seen seasons three, four, or five.

That would have been tragic.

The business insights from *Chuck* will be missed when the show comes to its scheduled end after a fifth season. But more importantly, I'll just miss the laughs, adventure and family fun offered in *Chuck*, a wonderful television series.

Thankfully, though, I'll have those *Chuck* DVDs to enjoy whenever I please.

About the Author

Ray Keating is chief economist for the Small Business & Entrepreneurship Council; a weekly columnist with Dolan Media Company (including *Long Island Business News* and *Colorado Springs Business Journal*); a former *Newsday* weekly columnist; and an adjunct professor in the MBA program at the Townsend School of Business at Dowling College. His work has appeared in a wide range of additional periodicals, including *The New York Times, The Wall Street Journal, The Washington Post, New York Post,* Los Angeles *Daily News, The Boston Globe, National Review, The Washington Times, Investor's Business Daily,* New York *Daily News, Detroit Free Press, Chicago Tribune, Providence Journal Bulletin,* and *Cincinnati Enquirer.* Keating also is a novelist, penning *Warrior Monk: A Pastor Stephen Grant Novel.* He lives on Long Island with his family.